The FRANCHISE Way

Basil Plews

authorHOUSE®

AuthorHouse™ UK Ltd.
500 Avebury Boulevard
Central Milton Keynes, MK9 2BE
www.authorhouse.co.uk
Phone: 08001974150

First published by AuthorHouse 7/10/2009

ISBN: 978-1-4389-9455-0 (sc)

This book is printed on acid-free paper.

Contents

Acknowledgements

My thanks are due to my sons, Tim, Andy and Nick for their support help and encouragement.

I am also indebted to Geoff Baxter M.A., BMus, PD-CHyp., MBSCH Clinical Hypnotherapist and Performance Coach for his invaluable chapter on 'Give Your Mind A Work Out.'

And, of course, to The British Franchise Association for their help and encouragement.

For her patience and understanding during the making of this book, I would like to dedicate it to my wife, Bev.

Introduction

Basil Plews was a successful businessman in his own right long before he had ever heard of the word 'franchise'. Having sold one successful family business, he was on the lookout for another that he and his son could manage together. Tim, of course, would be the one at 'the coal face', running it on a day to day basis with Basil in the role of guide and strategist, and so he took a long, hard look at the possibility of buying into a franchise. Bringing all the skills to bear that had made him successful in business, he evaluated a range of possibilities before settling on one that was to bring him the prestigious award of the annual Franchisee of the Year 2006 from Driver Hire Nationwide, itself the recipient of the award of Franchisor of the Year from the British Franchise Association in the same year.

And in this book, he has distilled the knowledge gained into the ultimate guide for those seeking to buy into a franchise.

Step by step, Basil takes you through the process of finding, choosing and running your successful franchise, setting you on the high road to success.

Welcome!

You have taken the first step to changing your life forever. When you read the following pages you will find they are full of real tips and techniques to bring the success that I have had to you and yours.

Do not think for one single minute that it is all going to be easy but one thing I will guarantee is that if you follow what I say it will be worthwhile. You will be absolutely clear about what you want to do, and in what kind of business you want to do it and importantly, how to do it successfully.

Every person has, by virtue of the fact we are here and alive, the opportunity to better themselves. Some of us go on to do more than that and there is nothing, nothing at all to stop you being as successful as anyone on this planet! Some may have had a head start, whether through schooling or personal contacts at certain levels. Good luck to them. Don't feel envious, feel fortunate that you have yourself together with that invaluable commodity – the will to succeed.

So let's work together through the pages, enjoy the experience and you will be armed with all of the tools that you will need to become very successful.

A little about me

I was what was known as a trouble-shooter. My function was to move into a business, live with it for a while and assess why a once successful business was now in trouble. There were all sorts of possible reasons, but that would take another book to tell you. After establishing what the downturn in the company was attributable to, a decision would be taken as to whether it was retrievable or not. If it was treatable I would carry on until the patient was in a fit state to look after itself once again.

I decided, for the reasons I will explain, and with the encouragement of my family and friends, to write this book.

The books on franchising that I have read have been extremely well written but I thought it would be interesting for you to read one written by a battle-scarred veteran of many years running his business as well as sorting out many other people's businesses.

Why, many would ask, did I, with all of this business experience, decide to go down the route of BUYING A FRANCHISE? Well, when after successfully selling a family business and my eldest son Tim had said, "Let's start something together dad," I thought "Here we go again! What-where-how.........?"

Why pay a franchise fee, and all of those hefty ongoing management fees? Why adhere to someone else's model, listen to some stranger's views and strategies on business? Because I wanted us to stand under someone else's business umbrella and buy into an already established brand. Even I, with my tried and tested experience, did not want or look forward to staring at a blank canvass. It gave me a warm feeling to know that we could, after finding the right franchise for us, reduce that long, lonely period and get much more speedily to the important bit: growing the business and, in turn, the bank balance.

This was a new one for me, having someone to ask questions of, and I knew they had probably heard them all before.

I decided to write this book to help you through the maze that is the world of franchising. Starting your own business is one of the most exhilarating and exciting times of your life. A chance to achieve and reach some goals you have only dreamed of.

I know I can help you succeed.

The UK Franchise Industry is
worth £12.4 billion

Self-employed on Cloud 9

There is a strong link between happiness and self-employment, says The British Franchise Association. Being self-employed can make a significant difference to an individual's general level of happiness. According to the latest survey from the British Franchise Association (bfa) in consultation with the Dean of the University of East Anglia's Business School, people running their own business are almost twice as happy with working life then people who are employed.

Yet the majority of respondents to the survey are not disposed to running their own business as 76% have never or seldom considered even starting one.

Those taking part in the poll were asked what they felt the main barriers were to starting their own business. Interestingly, the survey showed that the main obstacle to self-employment does not reflect a lack of interest but more a lack of means as 52% of respondents said that finance was an issue for them.

"Our research highlighted that 46% of those who run their own business are very happy at work as opposed to only 26% of those who are employed. Despite this there are a number of barriers to self-employment which could have very worrying implications for the SME sector and consequently, the UK economy," comments Dan Archer, Head of Marketing at the bfa.

He continues, "It is clear however that the primary concerns for self-employment are the financial investment involved and risk of business failure. It is here that franchising could play a vital role in boosting the confidence and economy of the UK. The nature of franchising is such that the risk of failure is significantly reduced as prospective franchisees operate a tried and tested system." This is reinforced by statistics from the NatWest/bfa survey which highlighted that over 90% of franchisees are profitable.

"When you consider the success rate associated with franchising, this can also lead to banks lending up to 70% of the total capital requirements, eliminating another start-up anxiety.

Franchising offers the opportunity to own and run your own business, backed by the security of a proven business model and the guidance of a franchisor support team.

Professor Nikolaos Tzokas, Dean of Norwich Business School, University of East Anglia, comments, "Interestingly the research shows that 'different strokes for different regions' may be required to overcome barriers to starting a business."

For example, in the Midlands, as compared to other regions, it seems that prospective entrepreneurs are more scared/have no confidence, and worried about failure rates. Building confidence and disseminating lessons from national and international successes and failures, among other things, should pay dividends in the Midlands. In London one should address, among other things, the considerable concern people have about the investment required for starting their own business and the fact that they do not know where/how to start up a business."

So what is franchising?

Everyone knows of McDonalds, perhaps the most widely recognised symbol on the planet, even if you're not a fan of hamburgers. And most people know that McDonalds is a franchise. But what exactly does that mean?

In plain terms, a franchise is an agreement of licence between two parties giving a person or group of people (**the franchisee**) the right to market a product or service using the trademark of another business (**the franchisor**). It's important to distinguish between the two, franchisor and franchisee.

Under this agreement the franchisee has the rights to market the product or service using the operating methods of the franchisor. The franchisee has the obligation to pay the franchisor certain fees and royalties in exchange for these rights. The franchisor has the obligation to provide these rights and generally support the franchisee. Strictly speaking, franchising is not a business but a way of doing business in which both franchisor and franchisee have a strong vested interest in succeeding and developing the business to their mutual advantage.

The franchises fall into several groups:

Management franchises where there is a business-to-business emphasis such as staffing and recruitment and secretarial services. Franchisors will usually expect the franchisee to have had some similar business experience and it will clearly require the employment of a workforce.

Retailing is a popular franchise where the significant advantages of trading under a readily recognised business logo can hardly be discounted. Staffing requirements may also be minimal, especially for a family-run franchise.

Job franchises are frequently one or two-man (or women) affairs such as plumbing, cleaning and car repairs, often making use of a van for deliveries or even as a portable workshop. This has the enormous advantage of often being able to be home-based with the consequent considerable reduction in overheads and is thus eminently suited to a husband and wife operation. These franchises tend to be the lower end of the investment scale.

Top of the list in terms of initial investment comes the investment franchise, typically seen in the management of name-brand hotels. Because of the large amounts of money involved, these are often managed by consortiums of business people.

Franchising may seem like an easy way to start one's own business and often will be, but investing in a franchise is no guarantee that you will be successful.

Your success in franchising will depend on three main factors: your ability to make the investment to secure the franchise and open it for business, the care with which you select the franchise, and, most importantly, your drive and ambition to make it successful.

So let's look at the pros and cons of the franchise business.

The most significant advantage is that you are not starting your business from the ground up. The franchisor has done all the heavy lifting, so to speak, and provided you with a name brand, public recognition through advertising and a tried and tested product or service. Just imagine trying to do this yourself with your own unknown brand or product.

There's no way to totally eliminate risk in business but franchising most certainly reduces the chances of failure. And never forget that your franchisor is every bit as anxious that you should succeed as you are.

Financing is also easier to obtain for an established franchise, banks being acutely aware that the prospects of success are far greater when there is an established brand behind the venture. And, even if your experience is limited, extensive training is included as part of your franchise fee and even better is the follow-up support that will be given by a good franchisor.

Most franchises ensure that you will have an exclusive territory. After all, there's little point in a franchisor seeing two of his franchisees battling for the same business.

So what's the downside?

Well, although you are working for yourself, as a franchisee you are not total master of your own destiny. Redesigning the company logo, for instance, is not going to make you popular with your franchisor!

And, of course, you will have to comply with whatever restrictions, rules or regulations they may see fit to impose. The amount of supervision you receive from head office will vary from franchise to franchise and, however much this may sometimes appear burdensome, always bear in mind that it is the systems and procedures laid down that have ensured the success of both their and therefore your business.

When there is a regular service charge involved, this can sometimes lead to resentment when the franchisee finds that he is leaning less and less on the franchisor for advice and support.

The inflexibility of the operation as detailed in the company manuals may irk those of an entrepreneurial nature, especially if the franchisor has become somewhat out of touch with the changing aspects of the business.

And there is the problem that the franchise you have chosen turns out to be not as advertised. I will come to that serious matter later on.

In the United Kingdom, there is no special legislation relating to the franchise business, the authorities considering that the present laws relating to trade to be sufficient protection. Hence the industry is virtually self-regulating and each individual franchisee would have to assess potential businesses for themselves.

In the late 1970s the British Franchise Association was formed to bring some sort of regulatory structure to a growing industry.

There were three categories of membership proposed:

- A full member
- an associate member for companies who are developing a franchise
- affiliate membership for lawyers, accountants, bankers and franchise consultants.

In addition, a 'provisional listing' is available for those franchisors that are at the early stage of their franchise development.

An applicant for membership must complete an application form and disclosure questionnaire which remains confidential to the bfa. A franchisor applying for membership must demonstrate that:

- The business itself is viable. The production of 24 months' recent and audited accounts will be required, including trading accounts, which shows that the business is capable of being run at a profit that will support a franchised network.
- The operating units in the business can be successfully replicated. The production of 12 months' recent and audited accounts is required for a managed arm's-length pilot franchise, or a fully fledged pilot franchise. These accounts must show a trading performance at least in line with the business plan set for the pilot franchise
- The contractual terms to be offered to prospective franchisees comply with the Association's ethical requirements. A copy of the then current

agreement and any changes thereto should be lodged with the Association

- The offer documents to be given to prospective franchisees present a full and realistic picture of the franchise proposition. A copy of the then current offer and any changes thereto should be lodged with the Association
- The franchise network has developed a viable number of franchised outlets. Continuity and longevity are key characteristics. In the case of an application for full membership, financial records should be provided to show that the franchised network is stable and profitable.

It can be seen that these provisos gave a good deal of security to franchisees signing up with a bfa-approved member. In their own words:

"One of the bfa's main jobs is to help potential franchisees recognise the good, the bad, and the ugly for what they are. Another is to help businesses involved in franchising to secure their own position amongst the 'good' operators.

"This work is not just a philanthropic exercise for reputable and responsible franchisors. It makes good commercial sense. The ability of franchisors to attract potential franchisees to invest in their systems depends crucially on their own reputation, and on the reputation of franchising in general.

"It was for these reasons that in 1977 the major franchising companies in the UK decided to set up their own association, the bfa, to act in the interests of the industry as a whole in assessing and accrediting franchising companies as those which meet its criteria for the structure of the business, the terms of the contract between franchisor and franchisee, the testing of the system and its success as a franchise.

"In the early days, franchising was concentrated in a limited number of markets, predominantly fast food, motor distributions and hotels, with a degree of uniformity in each section's structure and operation. Now at least 20 different business sectors are represented with insurance services; hairdressing to quick print and design, and video rental to roof thatching. Each business has its own variety of characteristics and its own pitfalls. Against this changing background, the bfa has developed standards to ensure that potential franchisees can continue to give credence to bfa accreditation."

Many franchises are not, however, members of the association, leaving potential franchisees to do their own 'due diligence' to assure themselves that they are making the right choice.

The statistics of the business make for an interesting reading. The following has been provided by the British Franchise Association.

General

- The franchise industry is now estimated to be worth £12.4 billion
- Over the past ten years the overall number of franchise systems has increased from 541 to 781, an overall growth of 44%
- There are an estimated 383,000 people employed by franchising
- The average (mean) turnover for a franchised business is £360,000
- The vast majority (93%) of franchisees say their

business is profitable
- The amount borrowed to finance a franchise varies greatly between different franchises. The average is £70,000
- Property services are now the largest sector. Business and commercial services is the second largest
- The internet is now the main recruitment channel, overtaking print press for the first time.
- 41% of franchisees use information sites, such as whichfranchise.com, when searching for information on franchisors
- bfa membership has also increased again with 45% of franchisors as members.

Relationships

- Relationships between franchisees and franchisors are healthy, with 86% reporting satisfaction in their dealings
- 71% of franchisors state the greatest hindrance to franchisor growth is the lack of suitable franchisees
- As many as 87% of franchisors are now using the internet as a method for recruiting new franchisees.

International Presence

- The number of British-run franchise systems with an international presence is 211 systems
- Europe is clearly the favoured destination for franchisors with just over a quarter (27%, up 2% on 2005) claiming to operate units on the continent
- The most common method of expansion is through granting a master licence (63%)

- Main barriers to overseas expansion are legislative requirements, desire to expand slowly, management's resources & language barriers.

Profile of Franchisees

- 81% of all franchisees are married
- The average age of a franchisee is now 47
- 66% of new franchisee recruits are male
- The personal services sector has the largest proportion of female franchisees at 58% compared with transport services which has 7%
- The number of graduates operating franchise units has increased slightly from last year to

  23%.

So you see that you are about to enter a booming industry.

But how to set about it? Here you should know a little about me and my background as I set out, along with my son Tim, to find a franchise that would work for us.

90% of all Franchises are still

profitable after five years

20% of new business start-ups

fail within twelve months

How it all began

It was a sunny day, an unusual event in the mining village of Bowburn County Durham and a strange day in my life as I walked through the gates of Bowburn secondary school for the last time. I was at the grand old age of 15 years and 1 month and free of the restraints of a school system that churned out factory fodder or, where I lived, largely pit fodder.

My father, who earned his money from the noble art of fighting or boxing, would say to me, "you are not going down the pit and you are not going into the ring." Well that left a slight dilemma: what am I going to do for a living? Football was my main interest apart from the full-time thoughts of our friends of the opposite sex. My parents had moved to London on doctor's instructions, and I was living with my Nan and Granddad, two of the nicest people in the world. I think it was seeing Granddad coming home to their tiny colliery house and sitting in the old tin bath in front of the fire, burning the coal he had helped dig up that gave me the will to have a different life, but it also gave me a work ethic that, when I came south, helped me through many hard and difficult times.

Saying goodbye to Nan and Granddad together with many aunties and uncles made the southbound platform at Durham station seem rather busy for a Sunday morning but in those times, especially in the north-east, it was the equivalent of emigrating to Australia.

I arrived at Kings Cross in the early evening to be greeted by my mum and dad and those other aunties and uncles who had also decided that the streets of London town were paved with gold.

The following morning I was escorted to an office at Ealing Broadway and duly interviewed by a Gestapo-trained man who chain-smoked throughout the interrogation and told me there were no jobs I could manage. Finally I was offered a choice of two jobs. Number one: servicing and repairing cookers, hair dryers, and transistor radios, or becoming an office boy.

The cluster of relatives, who of course had to accompany on that fateful day, sounded like some sort of choir – our Basil has to be White Collar not Blue Collar.
So the office boy it was.

That was the start of my adventure and *what* an adventure it has been. I would not have missed it for the world. That was a long time ago but yet it feels so recent.

By the time I was 28 years old, I was employing 450 men plus a number of administrative staff. Not too bad for a boy from a mining village in Co Durham.

I no longer have a desk and a chair at any given office but I have still got business interests with my eldest son Tim.

I have many differing types of investments and a solid residential and commercial property portfolio, so yes, I have been successful and I am going to share with you how I think that you can do the same.

I do wish the word FRANCHISE had hit the English dictionary in my younger days because, had it been, I would have got there in half the time.

The average amount borrowed to finance a franchisee is £70,000

A first look at franchising

Having been in business for many years myself, I had learned the hard way how difficult it is to start from ground zero.

It's not just a question of having the money, it's the long slow grind to develop whatever product or service you are selling until it becomes a viable and profitable entity. So when we looked for a new business that we could manage together, I felt it was time to look closely into the business of franchises, their pluses and their minuses.

Although I had read much about the process and could see the immediate advantages, there were still a good many unanswered questions in my mind and so we performed some serious 'due diligence' upon the available operations that we thought might be of value to Tim.

Then, at the first opportunity, we made a planned visit to the Franchise Exhibition at Olympia in London.

And one of the questions that has to be answered is: why do companies offer franchises in the first place?

By using the franchisee's money, a franchisor can expand his business. His staff, i.e. the franchisee, has a personal commitment to make it succeed and is responsible for the local management, leaving the head office free from many responsibilities. The disadvantage lies in the possible underperformance of a franchisee and so the vetting process to avoid this is stringent.

The first time Tim and I visited the Franchise Exhibition at Olympia it was a fascinating experience. Firstly, the number of companies exhibiting surprised me and on the London Tube the number of budding business owners on their way there surprised me even more.

You must remember when you read this that our situation was more relaxed than probably the majority of franchise seekers. We were there with no time restraints on starting up a new venture, whatever that would turn out to be. Yes, I preferred that it would turn out to be a franchise, for the reasons I have outlined earlier but if we could not find what we both thought to be the perfect franchise for us, so be it.

We were also in the enviable position of not needing to go behind the enemy lines of a bank to sell them the idea. We were friend not foe but I now know any meeting with a bank that has a department specialising in franchising is a massive bonus because they already have dealt with or will have all of the right questions that a franchisor worth his salt would be only too happy to answer to prove to the bank and their potential new business partner, the franchisee, that they were the correct commercial choice.

On the other hand the franchisor who is trying that bit too hard to shift territories that do not measure up commercially does not really want to be in the tricky situation of a question and answer session with either a bank or a potential franchisee who is armed with the right questions.

As the day progressed the biceps of a large number of visitors began to bulge under the sheer weight of the extra-strong plastic carrier bags they were hauling around this famous London venue. They must have collected enough information on buying a franchise to keep them busy for the next year. Their pre-exhibition preparation must have been virtually nil.

What a waste of their time and money, a day spent and for what? To fill up another recycling bin.

What about the exhibitors? I wonder what they think when someone wanders onto their not inexpensive exhibition stand with one arm dramatically longer than the other.

Attending a trade exhibition is fine but knowing what you are seeking there is paramount.

The preparation before such as this is all important – I have said how relaxed Tim and I were, but let me walk you through our preparation and, while you are reading this, remember if I were advising someone who did not have the experience that we have, my preparation would be even more in-depth.

Firstly we have to consider what would suit Tim's abilities and talents. Yes talents, for when we talk about a musician or an actor we talk about their talent. A businessman also has talent; you just have to find in which areas it falls. A musician may be talented in jazz and not in the genre of, say, heavy metal or rock and an actor might be better as a Shakespearian actor on the stage than in a TV sitcom.

"Know thyself" is a pretty good adage here – and no cheating!

So first you must decide: are you proactive or reactive?

Having run one of our businesses and been closely involved in the selling of it, I know that Tim was naturally very strong on dealing with the reactive side of business life. This was a major plus because we could now narrow down the franchisors we would approach. It would be a business that would require quick thinking on your feet. A business that would employ a number of people from day one. He is a real people person and loves to be around lots of other people.

Now we are ticking the boxes – a proven ability to work alongside other people in a tight environment, a few people working in the same office every day. Not a simple, straightforward task, especially if you are the boss, but I had seen Tim do it successfully.

Box two, thinking on his feet, no problem. Tim's a natural; you have got to be brutally honest with yourself about your own attributes. The successful people I have met over the years have used what some people would see as their own personal weaknesses and turned these to their advantage by concentrating on their strengths but, at the same time, never giving up strengthening the side of themselves they see as being weak. I think being aware is so very important.

The proactive side of any business is very important and although I said Tim was stronger on the reactive side of things, I maybe should have said he enjoys putting things right when they are going wrong, or making things better and even better when they are going well. Of course we will plan on advertising well in advance – we forward plan for staff – and of course sales always require forward planning.

Sales, I suppose, is a bit like having an allotment. You plan ahead and look after your soil, get rid of all of the weeds and then, and *only* then, when you know everything is in place and ready, do you start sowing your seeds. And even then as you are doing all of that back-breaking work, you know that the results of all of this work will not be seen for months. You are also uncomfortably aware that all of this could go wrong. You have done everything in the right order in the right way but many things outside of your control could come along and put paid to your efforts. So what do you do to reduce the chances of failure?

Let us now convert this into business terms – the base of most successful businesses is the people working in it, so the time you and staff invest in the franchisor's foundation course and all of the courses that are made available to you are of paramount importance. Not just turning up and going through the motions but lifting them up and bringing them back to your office with you. Don't forget these are tried and tested, so take full advantage of them. Also don't forget you have paid for these in your franchise fee so ensure that you get good value for your money.

If your franchise requires sales activity, which most will, then either you or your nominated sales person must invest as much time as you can make available.

When you achieve some success do not take your foot off the pedal because believe you me, unless you plant sufficient seeds you will not yield a good crop.

Think of all of this proactive time as an investment. You would not expect to plant a seed and it to grow and bear a crop immediately, nor would you expect to hand over a sum of money to the very best investment broker and for him to multiply it overnight; you would have patience in both these instances. Listen to your franchisor and ensure you have all the information you and your prospective client/customer requires.

Be absolutely certain the people who attend the sales courses arranged by the franchisor are the same people who will be going out on the road. I have seen on a number of occasions someone going on a course only to arrive back at their office and attempt to relay the information third-hand. It doesn't work and is a waste of time and money.

Now you have a solid base to work from and all of the homework has been done. You are ready.

Now you must have a plan. This is again where your investment in purchasing a franchise will pay more dividends. No doubt on the courses you have attended the word planning will have been used on numerous occasions. Never underestimate the value of planning because the result of *not* planning is failure, either in the long, if you are lucky, but more likely in the short term.

These companies that decided to franchise their already successful businesses know what they're talking about, their systems are tried and tested and this is one of the many reasons why you spent all of those hours deliberating whether it was the one to buy.

How long have they been going? Ask your friends and family, think about it day and night. Don't fall at this hurdle because many do. This happens for many reasons.

Some unsuccessful franchisees think: 'what we as a business are offering is so good and better than our competition all I have to do is to open the office and be available.' Wrong! What you have got to do is to take all of the information that has been given to you, plan a strategy, stick to it and do the same week in and week out, because this really works. The franchisor has given you his successful formula to succeed, so stay with it.

So why do these companies franchise if they have such a good product or service? Why give all of this away to some complete stranger?

There are many reasons. One is that they would find it difficult to employ individuals that would bring to the table the same enthusiasm and work ethic that a franchisee brings – or should bring.

Let's take the ideal franchisee.

A franchisee is investing his or her own money. And this is of course the fundamental difference; they will work the long hours that are required to make a financial success of their new business venture. Franchisees won't see long hours, they will look upon this as their investment in the future of themselves and their families.

They will have about them a built-in alertness, both in office hours and outside, that only someone who has embarked on this life-changing adventure can understand.

That thrill of starting the new business, the first weeks that turn only too quickly into months, watching all the work starting to convert itself into a commercial venture that *you* have created. The franchisor knows he would have found gold if he unearthed managers with the ethic I have described.

The good franchisors take their time and very carefully select from a proven template the type of individual they feel would suit their product or service and business culture.

One major player in the franchising would told me the perfect potential franchisee for them would be someone who had an entrepreneurial spirit that drives them ever onwards coupled with a strong work ethic and the will to be a team player.

An analogy springs to mind and that is Ferrari and McLaren. They build a Formula One racing car for you and a few others. They show every turn and gradient on the circuit, their team of engineers is available to you to answer any questions you may have, you have put in the hours studying the theory and you have done a few practice laps. Now it is time for you to actually race for real. It feels lonely at first but if you stick to the training, knowing it has worked for others, you will come through unscathed and feeling a sense of achievement that you would not have felt many times in your life before.

As each race goes by so your experience grows. That is what owning your own business is like, and with the added confidence of knowing you have a team around you with the expertise to guide you through any of the situations in which you may find yourself.

If you stick to the tried and tested formula, the good situations outnumber the bad.

The average turnover for a

franchised business is £360,000

The Toolmaker's Tale

There once was a man who was, without a doubt, the very best toolmaker that Vauxhall Motors had ever employed. Every night he would come home and tell his long-suffering wife the same thing: I am not appreciated, I am the best that they have; they don't know what they are doing; if it was not for me the production line would have come to a standstill – I should be working for myself but I suppose it's too late now – at my age, I have got to have a regular wage coming in!

Then one dark and dismal day the rain clouds really broke wide open when the dreaded news filtered down to the factory floor that all production was to be moved way up north. This included all R&D and, of course, the tool making division.

On arriving home that night, his wife thought he was unusually quiet, and he broke the news of his redundancy. The man was devastated, all those years spent with the one company, all of his friends, his life had been turned upside down. Where should he go to look for a job? This was new ground for him.

Doctors have stated that being made redundant is so traumatic it is only exceeded by divorce or death of a close family member.

His wife pointed out to him that he had said time and time again he should have been for working for himself – well here is the opportunity. Use the redundancy money and start your own business.

Off he went, bought all the machines he needed and rented a small workshop. He told a number of managers at the plant where he had worked what he was doing. Either the old managers got new positions with companies that required the skills of a good toolmaker or they had just spread the word but whichever, people started turning up at his house with jobs for him to do.

Before he knew where he was, he had to arrange for a telephone to be installed in his little workshop. There it was sitting on top of an old tea chest; the problem was it never stopped ringing. People were calling to either chase up delivery or to ask for a quote for the work they wanted doing. He was spending so much time on the phone or seeing people who turned up on spec – it was all getting out of hand.

Little did he realise at the time but he was being thrown into a world of which he had little or no knowledge, experience or expertise. All of those years on the factory floor had not prepared him for what was happening right now. The number of times he had sat in the canteen begging the question of his very eager listeners, as to what those guys who wear ties actually do with their time. Many times he had watched in envy when a tie made his way through the Hampton Court maze of machines on his merry way to the car-park to go to somewhere that always seemed to be a closely guarded secret. Now he was becoming a tie without a tie.

The tea chest was thrown out and a second-hand desk and chair was purchased and a simple partition built in the corner of the workshop to keep out the noise. Now things would be better. It was definitely more comfortable and quieter to be in a makeshift office but there was not much noise coming from the workshop because he was forever on the phone, and if he was not on the phone he was being kept away from the job by the many visitors who dropped in unannounced with potential work for him.

There was nothing for it, he had to employ someone to turn up every day to work for him; in fact to do what he once did, and then this would release him to do all of the things that were foreign to him. Deal with the VAT, the Inland Revenue, and the purchase ledger, answer the phone, order materials, do the wages for his employee, pay the bills, put on a clean tie and visit customers.

After a few months of doing all of this he was surprised that he was not getting orders from the many quotations that he had prepared, so he nervously approached a number of his contacts and asked them why.

He had not realised that there were so many other aspects to running a business than just the bit, albeit probably the most important, that his expertise brought to the table. It was this very expertise that encouraged the customers to choose him over some others. So when he vacated the workshop for the office he threw away the important edge he had over his competition.

He had no one to guide him through the business maze, admin courses, IT courses, sales etc. No one to talk to, and ask have you had this problem, have you had that problem. There is definitely some comfort in being part of a team, especially a team of like-minded people. When you talk to other franchisees remember that they are not and can never be competition because they, like you, have their own nominated area so in most cases they enjoy the contact with their fellow businessmen.

The moral of this tale is to stick to your strengths, do not jump head-first into something you are not equipped for or experienced in doing. Look further than your individual skills and realise that there is more to running a business.

This is why choosing the right franchise and franchisor pays dividends by taking care of all the ancillary tasks that make up a successful business.

You do not have to be Sir Alan Sugar or Sir Richard Branson to spot a need for a particular skill or service or product. You also have the added advantage of having the time to check out the success stories of the people who have already bought their franchises. Check out the areas that you feel are your weakest, it might be admin or IT, and run them past the franchisor – he will have dealt with them before, so do not be embarrassed to raise areas of concern about yourself. No one is an expert in everything.

Be honest with yourself. This is a long-term commitment and, if you follow my advice, you could become one of the other franchise millionaires.

Follow this step by step guide and you WILL be successful – and enjoy it!

66% of new franchisees are male

Average age 47 years

Try a bit of spying

Probably your first look at franchising will have come by way of the magazines devoted to the business or perhaps one of the websites listing various opportunities. In these you will see the glossy, alluring advertisements for franchises. But ignore the hype; look at the prospect with a clinical detachment.

I've already suggested guidelines for you to pick the business that will be within your capabilities. There's no point in attempting something which is either beyond your abilities, both professional and financial. An enormous debt load or a business beyond your skills or knowledge would be a recipe for disaster.

Here it's worth mentioning that running a franchise is not an exclusively male affair. Many franchises are equally, and in some cases, more suited to the feminine touch.

Having whittled the choices down to two or three or more, it's time to go and take a closer look.

As we did, the easiest place to start is at a trade show. But with the myriad of sparkling offers on display, it's easy to get waylaid and wind up with aching feet, a carrier bag full of useless brochures and a generally confused state of mind. You are visiting to see specific companies – just make sure that that's all you do!

But what you may be able to do after a visit to their exhibition stand is to eliminate one or two of your prospects. Perhaps they were too pushy, perhaps they were less than welcoming, and perhaps you just did not feel right about going into business with them. For remember, that is what you are contemplating doing. Your business is not going to be a solo effort, it will be a partnership every step of the way.

By the time you have shaken the dust of the exhibition hall from your feet, you should have at least a couple of likely prospects and, if they had been able to make a decision there and then, may well have arranged a visit to the companies in question at a future date. All well and good – but you might do better to go home and think over everything you've learned. A few days' contemplation will do no harm and whatever the franchisor has said to try and persuade you to make a decision on the spot, it's unlikely that the opportunity will be lost for the sake of a little time.

Now it's time for you to do some homework and a bit of spying to see how the land of the franchisee lies.

Visit different towns and cities and look at all different types of franchised businesses.

Look at every type of business that is available: fast food, retail, public houses, recruitment agency, estate agency, letting agency, printing cartridge shops, printing and countless more.

When Tim and I were looking we decided we needed to get more of a feel for what franchising actually meant, especially to the people who had actually bought one, so off we went to parts of the country we had never seen before. It would have been easy just to stick to areas we knew but to arrive in a town where you have not got a clue where anything is it makes you look everywhere and look at everything. You see things so very differently.

We chose to look at businesses that were transparent, the ones above. Of course, we started with the most difficult first – PUBS!

We all know what a pub is like, the sort of atmosphere in different types of pubs, the foodie pub, the country pub, the town-type pub and so on but do we know anything about the franchised pub? I did not and to be perfectly honest it had never been high on my list of priorities. Sure, when waiting to be saved from death from dehydration, but this was different.

So we bought a drink and found a seat, and with a certain amount of guilt, since we were the only ones who knew of our mission, started to take in the atmosphere. It was quite interesting because we were taking mental notes of things that under normal conditions would have gone unnoticed.

Was the owner (franchisee) relaxed, more efficient than in other pubs? The décor, how did that compare? And the staff, did they come across as customer-friendly? Because we as a country do not have the best reputation for customer service. It was very interesting because when we left, which was a bit of an effort, we started our box ticking and we both agreed that there was a definite formula running through the pub. One was that all the staff had the same polo shirts and that included the host. True, that is not unique to franchises but there was also the décor and general atmosphere ticking the boxes. Not scientific, I agree but after our first mission we were starting to become more aware.

Next stop, an estate agency. We looked at all the window displays of the independents, national chains and then the franchised operations. What struck us was that the franchised agencies had all the branding benefits of the multi-office agencies, but with the added ingredient of being run by its owner.

We stood in queues in everything from takeaways to printing and design shops, replacement cartridge shops and many more. Go and look for yourself. See the operation first-hand and that will be from the customer's point of view. Take note of any apparent differences between franchised and non-franchised operations, It will be of great help when you eventually sit down with any franchisor. They will appreciate the fact that you have put yourself in that situation, it gives them some idea as to what sort of people they will be dealing with. It is also a very simple and cost – effective way to start your homework.

It gives you a feel and you have to start somewhere, but of course, if you know which area of business direction you are pointed then you are more than halfway there.

93% of franchisees say their business is profitable

How we did it

We visited and trawled exhibitions, read every possible magazine and newspaper and all of the time we needed a template that fits over Tim. After all he is the one who is going to be daily at the coalface. It is no good thinking, yes that's the one for me, even if you may consider it to be the most successful one that you have seen so far – it has got to suit you, your personality, your character, your staying power and your interests. I cannot stress this strongly enough.

Let me try and give you an example on how you might go about settling on a franchise. "I love cars," he might say – so that sounds simple enough until we start looking a bit deeper and I ask a few questions. He says: "I would not like to have anything to do with engines, when I say I like cars I don't mean messing around with oil or the engine." Easy then, something to do with the sale of cars or perhaps their financing. "Oh no," he says, "I don't want to go to work wearing a suit and tie, that's what I'm trying to get away from."

OK, it doesn't sound like it but we really are starting to get somewhere, now we are narrowing down the field. One option could be dent repairs – you would have your business clients who would want the little dents and knocks repaired on their part-exchange vehicles and of course you would also have the public contacting you directly from your advertising. Windscreen repairs are another business with both business and private users.

This is also useful – spreading your business across the private and business sectors. The profit in the private sector will be greater then the commercial; also payment will be immediate where you may have to give credit terms to large dealerships, so having the two sides to the business helps. I doubt that a Ferrari, Aston Martin or BMW dealership will run to their accounts department to raise a cheque for you, but once they become a customer you will have a regular call pattern, so that is the upside to the business customer compared to the private.

I have used the above example but you could apply the same principle to many types of business.

Back to Tim. After looking into Driver Hire's operation, a company set up to supply temporary commercial drivers as an agency; no different to any recruitment company supplying temp staff, such as typists, it looked promising. We started from the outside, looking at the Yellow Pages from different areas of the country, speaking, as best we could, to a number of transport companies to get their opinion about the credibility of the company. We then spoke to anyone we knew who had any knowledge about lorry driving, van drivers, etc. We then did a check at Companies House just to see what financial substance they had. It showed a company with an annual turnover of about 65 million pounds and about 80 franchised offices.

So far so good. The next step was to visit their offices in Yorkshire. We met their chairman and other directors where they explained their operation. It was, I am very pleased to say, made clear to us that they were extremely careful as to who was allowed to buy a Driver Hire franchise.

At this point in our research you must ask yourself 'do I get along with these people, do I trust them – will I enjoy working with them?' Note everything, even down to the way you were dealt with when you arrive at their reception area. Take all of the information that you are given but do not start to look at it there and then unless they would like to run through it with you. Ask them what they prefer to do. They should be happy to give you time to read and absorb their material.

Ask them about visiting other franchisees, which ones they do recommend or can you choose for yourself. In the case of Driver Hire they gave us a complete list of names and addresses and told us to choose two or three that were convenient to us. Another box ticked.

We eventually chose Driver Hire as our preferred option and fortunately they felt the same way about us.

So we now start to look for premises. Good franchisors will help you with this task as they have had years of experience doing it for others. They will also advise you on leases and so on. If you need help with funding they will help as well, in preparing management accounts, cash flow forecasts for the bank and advise on many of the problems associated with producing a business plan.

Now come the courses: sales, IT, compliance, ISO, insurance, marketing, finance and more besides. And there are some of the benefits of buying a franchise – provided it's the right one for you.

From Driver Hire we bought a 'green fields' operation, i.e. a brand new operation. Our first cheque was for £83.25 and Tim photocopied it and had it framed. Fours years later, our turnover was around £1 million.

Five years later the Driver hire Nationwide Network had expanded to 107 offices and awarded our office the Franchisee of the Year for 2006 in the same year Driver Hire nationwide won the British Franchise Association Franchisor of the Year award; quite an achievement.

So it proves that it does work if that you make your choice of franchise wisely. But you must work at it every day with the same enthusiasm as if it were your first. I will go into this a bit later.

An estimated 383,000 people are now employed in franchising

So, is it for you?

It may be that working on your own is not for you. You will of course have the comfort of knowing there is always someone to call but it can still get lonely. The franchisor can only spend a limited amount of time with each one of his franchisees.

Speak to as many people as you can. Ask them to try to think of as many negatives as positives. If you have always had a wage hitting the bank on a regular basis you must try to put yourself in the situation of imagining what it must be like to succeed or fail on your own. You must know some self-employed people; I am not suggesting you compare types of jobs, careers or lifestyles but just try to get a flavour of the world of the self-employed.

But if you do go it alone and get it right, and there is no reason in the world why you should not, it is a great feeling. Satisfaction. Self-respect. Your business life will become part of you and you will grow into one another. Building your future for your family. There will be difficult times but when aren't there? The trick to all of this is choosing the right franchise for you. Homework and more homework.

One other important point is your understanding of the structure of what is effectively your business partner, the franchisor. He will probably put in place regional or area business development managers (BDM) or similar. Their function is to ensure the franchisees in their region have everything at their disposal for the smooth running of their businesses. The BDM will also be responsible for regular reports on your attitude towards the new systems or changes in products and services provided by group or head office.

The BDM, or his equivalent, is there to help and provide a link between you and everyone else involved. If, for instance, you have just been on a course, say for sales or compliance, he will make one of his regular visits to ensure you are comfortable and fully understand the why, when and wherefore. But never forget that he is there to increase turnover and obviously will always look at your margins, just as you should do on a weekly basis. I know some franchisees who monitor their operations daily and why not? With today's technology it is not the major task some seemed to think it was in the not too distant past.

Treat your BDM in the way you would like to be treated yourself. He can become a good friend and remember he wants just the same as you – SUCCESS. He is a mine of invaluable information. If you have a particular problem, put it to him, for no doubt on his visits to other like-minded franchisees within his area, he has come across the same or similar situation and undoubtedly the answer was found. If he cannot come up with a solution, I would wager one of his colleagues covering a different part of the country will.

In a franchise YOU ARE NEVER ON YOUR OWN.

But to make it work YOU MUST BE A TEAM PLAYER.

So, do you know yourself? Here's a simple questionnaire for you.

It is essential that you take time to consider your own strengths and weaknesses, before you enter into serious discussion with any franchisor. Work your way through the following and see how you measure up.

First assess your abilities:
- Does the franchise allow you to exploit your natural aptitudes, skills and strengths?
- Are you at your best performing mental tasks?
- Are you at your best doing physical tasks?

Then see what demands the proposed franchise will make on you.
- Will your age and health permit you to run the business long enough to recover your investment and make the effort worthwhile?
- Do you have the ability and commitment to work hard, often during unsociable hours?

Now see how your family measures up:
- Does your family support your venture?
- Will your family cope with the demands of the business on your time?
- Will any of your family be able, or willing, to help you?

Think about money:
- Do you have sufficient resources to get a business off the ground and survive the initial start-up

phase?
- Could you cope with any losses or unexpected setbacks while building the business?
- Are you prepared to put your assets at risk?
- Can you raise sufficient finance?
- Can you do the job?
- Do you understand franchising principles and what is involved?
- Do you believe you have the physical and mental temperament to work for yourself?
- Will you be able to handle staff?
- Can you accept the discipline of a franchise system, including the franchisor's authority?
- Would you be better off becoming self-employed through an alternative route?
- Can you achieve what you are looking for through this venture?

Once you've completed this, talk it over with a friend or family member. It is important to take your time at each stage of this process. Remember there is no shortage of franchises to choose from and thus no reason to make a hasty decision that you may later regret.

Property services is now the

largest sector of franchising

Give your mind a workout

As you're undoubtedly anxious for me to get on with the nuts and bolts of getting your franchise, you are probably going to skip this chapter! But, if you do, I suggest you come back to it later as it can be an invaluable aid to self-assessment. You might surprise yourself!

We are all becoming increasingly aware of what we want to get from life. We are much more likely to change aspects of our life that we are not happy with and it is clear that our ability to define and maintain the right career exerts a major impact on our quality of life and our own success. The old model of a job for life in which we climb the career ladder gradually is, in many cases, outdated and so it may be that franchising gives you the opportunity to regain an element of control over your life while still giving the comfort of an established brand and support network.

You are reading this book because you are considering making a significant career change and see franchising as a way of facilitating that change. This chapter deals with some of the psychological and emotional issues surrounding this important decision. We will examine some of the reasons for embarking on this new career and identify some of the elements of successful and satisfying careers.

By the end of this chapter you will have begun to acquire the skills that will enable you to create your own road map to a new career and there are some exercises you can try in order to establish positive thought patterns. It is useful to develop skills of self-assessment so we will look at a few ways of identifying traits in yourself and learning new skills. We will go on to look at ways of developing your mind in order to be able to relax, think clearly, focus attention, set goals and continue your personal development.

Preparation

Firstly let's look at some of the reasons for considering a new career. There are a few possibilities and it is important to identify why you feel that a career move is important in order to clarify the direction in which you want to move.

- It may be that you find that earlier in life you embarked on the wrong career entirely, either through a mistaken idea of what the job entailed or through outside influence e.g. parental pressure. You may have stayed in a career that doesn't fit through habit or financial pressures
- Perhaps you just find your current job unsatisfying in some respects - you may have acquired new experience that makes your job less satisfying. Or maybe your industry or company has changed requiring you to adapt or retrain to continue in your current role

- You may feel that as time has passed you have changed within yourself and your priorities in life have changed
- Perhaps you love your work but interpersonal relationships within your company or team make it difficult or impossible to remain where you are.

One of those descriptions may fit your circumstances perfectly or it may be that there are several elements that are relevant to your current situation. Whatever the reason, it is essential to have a clear idea of why you want to make a change in your working life.

The next step in our road map to a satisfying career is to identify the key features that lead to job satisfaction.

People who love their work:
- Feel valued
- Are dedicated
- Apply themselves enthusiastically to tasks
- Invest huge amounts of energy in work
- Do what needs to be done no matter how personally draining
- Welcome new challenges and responsibilities.

To further investigate the features of job satisfaction we must also look at some of the key elements.

- Mental: Do you feel stimulated and excited by your individual role?
- Emotional: Do you feel that you are doing something worthwhile? Are you aware of the greater good of what you are achieving for your family, community or society as a whole?
- Practical: Do you have to commute to work? Do you miss out on family life and free time, do you

find the journey itself stressful and draining before you even begin work? Do you have to drive, operate machinery, sit in front of a computer, or work in an uncomfortable environment?

• Control: How much control do you have over your work life? Are you left to make your own decisions or is every move dictated by someone else? Are you responsible for a team or are you independent? Are you part of a clearly defined structure or are you sometimes unsure of your exact role?

Think about what you really get from work. What role does work have in your life, does it just pay the bills or is it the thing that really drives you? Now identify what role you would *like* work to have. Really be honest with yourself. If it is just to have a nice lifestyle then are you really willing to devote the time and effort to establish your new business? When setting up a new business it is important to identify your key reasons for doing this. This is a vital step in getting a handle on your own motivation. It is not enough just to say 'I want to make money'. What do you want to make money for? Is it for the family? Is it so you can start a family? Is it so you can retire early or is it so you can afford a lifestyle you have imagined? All these ideas are a starting point but they are not enough to establish and maintain a business. The business will not just make money because you have decided you want it to. For the business to make money it must be successful and for the business to be successful you must devote and continue devoting attention and energy to it.

So what are some of the features of a franchise? Let's look at some of the key advantages of franchises and also be realistic about the potential disadvantages.

Control- the most obvious difference with a franchise-based business is control. Moving from a structured skill-orientated job to a franchise offers you the opportunity to be involved in every aspect of the business. It is, after all, *your* business. That means that your efforts are directly related to the satisfaction you feel in yourself and the success of the business

Financial- there are potential financial advantages and, although this is not guaranteed, franchises have a much higher success rate than conventional start-up businesses.

Part of established structure- although you are your own boss you are part of an existing structure and this structure will have been shown to be successful in existing franchises.

Proven track record- you can look in to the success rate of existing franchises within the company you choose and see that these businesses have succeeded.

Strong support network- the company will have invested time, effort and finances in getting you started so it is in their best interests for your business to succeed. You will have access to people who understand the situation you are in and the benefit of their expertise.

With a franchise there is no need to establish a brand- you have no need to invest the huge time and resources that it takes to launch a new brand on the marketplace. Franchises will, in many cases, have an established recognisable brand and their own marketing team will be raising the profile of the company.

Be realistic about what you hope to gain from a move into a franchise-operated business. As with all things you must be aware of the potential disadvantages. There is, of course, the uncertainty of moving from a salary to a lack of fixed income. You will be your own boss but will still be held within clear constraints and structures with your own responsibilities and obligations. You primarily have a responsibility to the franchisor and their investment of time and resources in you, and you ultimately have the responsibility for ensuring that the business succeeds. You may also be moving out of your own personal comfort zone, perhaps moving from a narrow focus or technical orientation to having wider responsibilities over many aspects of the company, such as finance, stock, cash flow, staff, HR, payroll, accounts and marketing. Remember that we get satisfaction from new challenges so embrace these new responsibilities. Your payback for this effort is that when your business is successful you can take a huge amount of satisfaction from the fact that you were instrumental in making that happen. You also get to feel that you are directly rewarded for your efforts in that you are working for yourself rather than the company.

Self-assessment and emotional intelligence

We have discussed how successful and satisfying businesses require huge amounts of attention, dedication and enthusiasm, so in considering a franchise it makes sense to enter into a business in which you are in some way interested. One that you know you can be driven by. In order to make an educated decision about which franchise to operate it is important to get as much information as you can. The first step in this quest is gaining information about yourself - insight into what makes you tick. In order to choose the right career path for you it is essential to correctly identify what drives you and what gives you satisfaction.

It is obvious that we are all different. We each have our own unique personality, our own traits, our own skills. But it is important to realise these traits are not fixed. We are not genetically predisposed to be any sort of person. Obviously our direction in life is influenced by the opportunities that are open to us but that does not mean our destiny is preordained. It just means that it may take more effort to move in one direction than another. It is useful to realise this because it means that you can identify any changes you would like to make in your own thought patterns and you *can* actually make these changes. You can become the person that you want to be. We are all a product of our experiences and most of what goes on in our minds is a product of the behaviour we have learned in our lives. Once you have accepted that fact then you know that you can learn new, more positive ways of thinking and new, more positive ways of behaving. It's not about changing personality but changing the emphasis of the elements of your personality. Learn emotional intelligence in order to use your own mind more efficiently.

We generally accept that for things to warrant merit they must have taken a huge amount of effort but just because it is difficult does not mean it is worth that effort. It is true that we appear to gain satisfaction from things that have taken effort to achieve but we need to learn to use our energies efficiently - to learn when we can change and control a situation and to learn when we just need to accept it. It is also useful to realise that events in themselves are not inherently stressful. It is how we react (our emotional intelligence) that dictates the effect on us. The important thing to realise is that although we may not be able to control everything in our lives we can learn to control our reactions and the impact these situations have on us. Some things happen without planning i.e. by chance. We must also be able to adapt to these changes and be able to use them to our advantage and incorporate the results of such developments into our future plans.

We have laboured under the misapprehension that processing huge amounts of information is the way to professional success. Intelligence and skills relate to information are of limited use if we cannot develop the emotional skills to interpret the information and implement change and work well with others and communicate.

So, it is important to develop self-assessment skills. By finding out more about yourself you can find out what your strengths and weaknesses are and identify any changes you would like to make. Awareness of your own personality helps you to react to situations in a way that you control rather than just through habit. It also informs your perception of others and helps you empathise with the position they are in.

Conduct a personal interview with yourself as if you were being interviewed for a job. In this interview be very honest with yourself. Start by concentrating on your strengths.

Your Personal Interview
- List those strengths on which others rely on in you at work.
- List the responsibilities you have at work.
- List the achievements of which you are most proud in your personal and professional life.
- List the things your friends and family like about you.
- List the personality traits you are most proud of in your self.

- List the improvements you could make in yourself. Do not see these as faults but as elements of your life that you seek to improve.
- What would you like to change about yourself?
- What would you like to be better at?
- What do you like about work?
- What do you dislike about work?
- Describe your ideal job.
- What would you really like to do?
- What job would you really be suited to?
- Where would this job be?
- What industry would it be in?
- Would it be related to your existing career?
- Would it be something completely new and different?
- Would it be based outdoor or indoor?
- What are your interests, hobbies, and passions?
- What did you used to do in the past that you really enjoyed?
- What have you always wanted to do?
- Describe running your own franchise.
- What do you think it would give you?
- What are the advantages and disadvantages?
- Which of your personality traits might suit a particular franchise?

When you have conducted your interview you should have a clearer idea of what you want from your career and what kind of job will give you the satisfaction you desire. You should also have an insight into the strengths and weaknesses you see in yourself and what others see in you.

As previously mentioned it is important to see our personality as constantly changing and influenced by experiences and it is an important step in self-awareness to identify changes we want to make in ourselves. Our personalities and thought patterns are not fixed and we can learn to control our thinking. Become an optimist. This is an essential step in motivating yourself. If you don't believe you can do it then what is the point in even trying? In every task use positive self-talk. Even if you don't quite believe the positive things that you tell yourself, just do it anyway. Positive thoughts will gradually erode any old negative thought patterns.

The first step towards achieving any personal or professional goal is telling yourself you can do it and actually believing it. Develop a constructive internal dialogue. When you develop this positive self-talk you cultivate a new positive way of thinking and positive thinking allows you to take positive action. When you tell yourself you can't do it then you can't. You have decided on failure before you even begin. So instead, even if it takes effort, tell yourself 'I can', 'I will', 'I am'. Study the examples of positive and negative self-talk and see if you recognise any statements in your own language. Make a note of any other negative self-talk you use and choose positive statements to replace it.

Positive self-talkNegative self-talk

I canI can't

I will I won't

I am I hope

I'm greatI might

I have good ideasIf only

I make a positive impactWhy can't I?

I'm strongI should

I'm in controlI must

I make things happenI should have

I'm intuitiveI failed

I'm assertiveI'm stressed

People respect my opinionsI can't cope

I'm a valued workerPeople don't respect me

I'm experiencedI'm a failure

I learn from mistakes

I'm positive

I'm relaxed

It is of the utmost importance that you listen carefully to what you tell yourself. What you tell yourself is what you believe. Whatever anyone else says about you, your own opinion of yourself is by far the most important. So from now on listen to what you tell yourself and always think, 'is that really what I want to hear? Is that the best advice I can give myself?'

Be self-aware and ask yourself at various times during the day, 'what am I feeling now? What do I want to feel? How am I behaving? How do I want to behave? Am I making any assumptions? What do my senses tell me?'

It's also a useful exercise to involve someone else in your internal dialogue, someone you really care about, and give him or her the best advice you can. Imagine the things you tell yourself are directed at them. Think to yourself: 'is that the best advice I would give to someone I care about?'

Also invent a kind of internal advisor or mentor. Picture someone whose opinion you really respect. It can be a colleague, family member, historical figure, even a fictional character, but get an image of that person and hear them giving you the advice you would like to give yourself. At all times remember that you have decided to only allow positive thoughts. Ask yourself, 'how would my mentor feel in this situation? How would my mentor behave in this situation?'

Goal Setting and Motivation

Now that you have conducted some research into yourself and the concept of making a career change it is very important, in order to motivate yourself, that you set goals and continue to strive for success. Goal setting is very important because in order to achieve what we want to in life we must have a very clear idea of the direction in which we want to move. So here is a simple 12-step plan for setting goals, achieving them and continuing to motivate yourself.

1.   Develop a desire
2.   Develop a belief that it is possible to achieve
3.   Write it down
4.   List benefits
5.   Define starting point
6.   Set deadlines
7.   Ascertain obstacles
8.   Research your topic and find out what extra information is needed. Test alternative career choices. Find out more about your chosen franchise. You can take leave from your current job, get some training, help

out in a related business, try out new projects alongside your current job, do voluntary work

9.   Find someone who can help. If you are a high achiever it may be difficult to admit to something you can't do but remember we are always learning and can always gain from someone else's experience. Find someone with specialist experience in your chosen field or just someone who gives good advice. Remember that there is always someone who has been in the same position and faced the same challenges

10.   Plan

11.   Visualise

12.   Never give up.

Setting achievable goals is essential in taking a structured approach to developing your career. Set goals for days, weeks, and months but also decide what you want to do with your career. What is your ultimate goal? Decide what you really want and remind yourself regularly what that goal is. Every day think about what you need to do to bring that goal closer.

Define the pros and cons of a new career. Remember that by setting goals they are not rigid and fixed. They can adapt and change and it is likely that goals change as you gain experience and information and as your perceptions and priorities change. Have an overall plan but remember that the plan can be fluid. We learn by doing so you will be better equipped to set the next goal as your mind absorbs new information and experiences. Every small step is important because even if it is not the correct move it will inform the next one.

To achieve your own peak performance level you must aim high. Have a dream and set a large-scale but ultimately achievable goal for yourself. Have inspirational people around you to give you advice and motivate you. At all times try to exceed your previous personal best performance. As well as keeping an eye on the bigger picture you must ensure that you take every step carefully along the way. You must really focus and be aware of every last detail, understand every aspect of your new business and prepare for every eventuality. Remember that achieving your peak performance is easier than maintaining it so you must continue to motivate yourself along the way. Your own success and satisfaction are interlinked so ensure you keep setting goals for yourself. Motivation is the pursuit of a goal so you must always be pushing yourself.

Conclusion

So what we have come up with is a road map for changing your career and grasping new opportunities. Let's review the key steps.

1. Find out why you want to change your current job. What is wrong with it? Do you feel undervalued? Underpaid? Unsatisfied? Is it a logistical decision? Are you required to move? Have you changed? Has the company changed?

2. Imagine your ideal job. Really take some time to think about this. Once again think about every aspect of it: mental, emotional, and practical. Where would you like to work? What kind of environment would you like to work in? How much would you like to earn? Which industry would you like to work in? Do you want a career related or far removed from your current one?

3. Clarify the notion of what this ideal job really is. Does this ideal job really exist? Get some help. Speak to people who might be doing similar things. See if their experience matches your perception. Find out if the reality of your idea matches the

fantasy
4. Research. Research as much as you can. Interview anyone whose opinion may be useful. Get experience. See if you can test out your career by helping out in someone else's business, getting training, working part-time, taking leave from your current job
5. Work out the pros and cons of the decision you are making. Consider all aspects of the decision: changing career; starting a franchise; working for yourself
6. Don't let fear of the unknown be the only thing that stops you
7. Set goals. Once you make the decision to start a franchise set clear goals for yourself and your business. The first goal is when you want to start it, when you want to leave your current job. How do you want the business to develop? How much do you want to turn over in the 1st year and 2nd year etc? What proportion of the potential business in your area do you want to have in the 1st year and 2nd year etc? In order to guarantee future satisfaction always continue to set goals for yourself and for the business. Never be tempted to rest on your laurels. Never allow yourself to be complacent about your business
8. Be self-motivating. Take stock of your personal well-being. Be aware of new positive traits you have found in yourself. Only allow positive thoughts and look forward to your next achievement. Enjoy the justifiable pride you feel in setting and achieving goals.

By reading this book you have already taken your first step forward. You are researching your subject and gathering the information you need to make an informed decision. In this chapter you have learned to take a structured approach to this potential career change. You have also learned the importance of finding out about yourself and taken the first steps towards learning how to relax, focus and motivate yourself. Hopefully this information will clarify some of your own ideas and help you move into a new and satisfying business.

41% of potential franchisees use information sites, such as www.whichfranchise.com, when searching for information on franchises

The downs and the ups

The downside to buying and running a franchise

The franchisor is in control. You must buy all stock-in-trade from the franchisor. This can apply to many different types of franchise, such as: restaurant, food takeaway and many types of retail

Management fees. These are ongoing, linked to turnover, and can vary but be anything between 5% to 30%.

Some franchisors might make bad decisions or not make decisions at all, not keep up to speed with the competitors, or fail to update procedures or services.

The original contract between you could be far too restrictive. You only find this out if and when you come to try to sell the business.

There may be other parts of the contract that restrict you in other ways; what you know now, you did not know then.

Get as much advice as you can before you sign what is usually a five-year agreement, renewable with both parties' blessing.

The upside of franchising

- You get full training, with no previous experience needed
- Your very own exclusive area
- You join a proven successful business
- You get an established brand name, products or services
- Banks are far more likely to loan money to you because of a successful history dealing with that business sector and that particular franchisor.

The banks are a good gauge as to the credibility of a franchisor. They will be unlikely to fund a business that has a poor financial track record, so the banks are always a worthwhile port of call; it is in both your interests.

By now I'm sure you have a load of questions or concerns, so here are a few answers to the most common ones.

Q I am worried about keeping up to date with all of the regulations.
A The franchisor will keep you up to date with all of the rules and regulations affecting your industry. This will leave you free to run your business and make money.

Q Do many people who buy a franchise fail?
A Franchising has become a great way to start a

business, with less than 1% failure rate and over 90% of franchisees in profit.

Q How do I choose the franchise for me?
A As I have suggested, look at your own personal interests and what types of natural abilities you have. It is also important to line this up with an industry that has plenty of potential growth. Look at reports published by global research company Mintel to identify the markets that are growing. In 2006 their report on eating out stated that home-delivery food was the fastest growing segment of the eating-out market. They will also indicate who the major players are in any given market.

For inspiration take a look at the bfa Franchisor of the Year Awards. Entrants for the top award have to demonstrate how they are responding to consumer needs with new systems, products and services. The Brand Builder of the Year Award recognises a franchisor that has supported and added value to its brand during the last year.

Q If I am still not certain is there anything outside of the box I can do?
A Yes there is. In certain industries, the franchisor will allow you to actually work for a few days or even weeks in one of his operations. I have seen this work very successfully in the food industry. Some franchisors encourage this to happen as it also ensures that you are making the right decision.

Make your quest for finding a franchise into a fact-finding mission to become the expert on the franchise industry. I guarantee that all of the effort you make will pay massive dividends in the future.

To look into the industry costs you virtually nothing apart from your time and I can assure you it will be one of the best investments of your time you have ever made.

Q How much money can I borrow from the banks?
A A guide, and this is *only* a guide, is that you have £30,000 of capital to invest. A bank with a dedicated franchise department will lend you a further £70,000 therefore giving you start-up capital of £100,000.

Meeting with your franchisor

You will notice that I am always emphasising the fact that this will be a partnership. You are not going to be working alone and thus it is vital that you appreciate the value of teamwork. It's one of the things that the franchisor will be looking for at the interview. Enthusiasm and initiatives are welcome, mavericks are not.

Unlike your meetings on the exhibition stand, this will be much more a two-way street. The franchisor will still be in a selling mode but in this case you will have to be also. For while this is your opportunity to nail down some hard facts concerning the prospective opportunity, they will be looking to nail down some hard facts about you.

Even though you will be handing over some hard cash to them, this will be little compensation to them should you fail to make the business work. And you are not buying a business, you are leasing it and the relationship is much more akin to that of landlord and tenant.

Don't rely upon your memory; the fact that you can be seen to be taking notes only confirms to them that you are a serious prospect.

When I have been asked in the past by people as to what sort of questions to ask, I have given them a sort of shopping list to get them started.

Keeping it very simple yet trying to get to the heart of the matter is crucial.

It's well worthwhile taking a copy of this along to your meeting and noting the answers to your questions in the space provided for review later. I have added a 'cut out and keep' copy of this at the end of the book.

1. Are you members of bfa and if so what type of membership? If you are not a member, why not? (Remember the greatest percentage of franchisors are not members of the bfa)

2. How long has your company been trading and how long have you been franchising?

3. What is the number of existing franchisees and how do you split areas (by postcode, per head of population, households)? In some instances it can be beneficial to get involved with a franchise just starting out, because you have the pick of the areas available. The franchise purchase fee may be fairly low at this stage as well but because it is new it is unproven as far as franchising is concerned, therefore may constitute a higher risk than an established franchisor. Also, if you need to borrow from a bank, they will be less favourably inclined towards a franchisor with no established record of success.

4. The training. Where will it take place; in the classroom or in the field? Is it ongoing? Apart

from the obvious training regarding the product or service, does it cover, say, administration, financial management, marketing, IT etc?

5. Do you have a national sales force and what sort of help do I get in my area? Do you open doors on a national head office basis? And then would I be expected to approach individual regional offices within my area? Apart from your national advertising and literature, am I helped in any other way?

6. Point out a number of areas of the country and ask how long the franchisees have been with them. Do they turn down many potential new franchisees and if so why? What are they looking for in a new franchisee?

7. Is the area exclusive to me? How long will the franchise agreement run for and how is it renewed? Give me a couple of actual examples. Have you ever refused to renew and why?

8. How much is the initial franchise fee? What is the ongoing management fee? Are there any other fees?

9. Do you have a sample copy of the franchise agreement for me to take away and study (it would be usual at this stage for you to sign a confidentiality agreement)?

10. Do you have a sample forecast of projected turnover for the first five years? How about the projected profit for the same period?

11. Can I sell my franchise on the open market and, if so, can you help? (Remember a successful franchisor will probably have a strong brand, therefore putting you in a good position in the marketplace if you decide to move on). Also, question worthwhile asking is: can you move it on to a close family member?

Once you have left the meeting, it's time to go over your notes and evaluate very carefully what you have learned. Here are a few suggestions of questions to ask yourself:

1. Have you enjoyed the meeting?
2. Could you picture yourself working alongside them, talking regularly on the phone, attending national conferences, regional meetings etc?
3. Were they being in your opinion a bit over-optimistic? Did you have a feeling they were a bit over-keen to recruit you as a franchisee?
4. A good and successful franchisor is extremely selective as to who joins his team. Were they?
5. What am I getting for my money? The initial fee (the franchise fee) generally covers the following:

Training	yes	no
Help with initial advertising	yes	no
Supply of some equipment	yes	no
Help with finding premises	yes	no
Help with staff	yes	no

The franchise fee does not generally provide profit stream for the franchisor. It is there to recover costs relating to the above and contribute to their setting up costs of the initial operation. Their profit will come in the longer term from management service fees. These fees do vary but the following is an actual example:

Say the management fee is 10%. This can be broken down as:

6% to the head office of the franchisor

3% to regional back-up

1% to advertising fund.

Some franchisors do not include advertising in the management fee, they charge separately for it. Make sure that you have ascertained this point.

So you now have the questionnaire you filled out at the meeting with the franchisor and your own notes on your reactions to the meeting. Bearing in mind all the previous advice on the selection of a franchise, you should now be in a good position to make a considered decision.

Undoubtedly, provided you have impressed with your potential to succeed, you will be asked to make a decision there and then. But, once again, a period for contemplation would be wise and you need time to study the contract. Take your completed check list home and study it carefully, then fill in the post-interview check list.

All looking good?

Great, now we're in business.

The franchise relationship

Here we should look at just what will be the crucial factors in your relationship with your franchisor. Clearly a franchise is a great way of starting and running a business, reducing the risk factor associated with a start-up considerably. But to make it work, you must be aware of the position of the franchisor.

It's really a curious business relationship. Apart from the obvious goodies covered by your franchise fee, it does not buy you a business, merely the right to do business in the name of the franchisor. And equally, you are not the employee but will be acting in the best interests of the company and will own the outlets for the goods and services they are providing.

If you have high expectations for success, so will your franchisor. His aim is to expand his company and that is what he will be looking to you to do for him. Anything less than a harmonious relationship will fail on both counts.

You have met your future partner and got the answers to the questions in the last chapter. Now it is time to sit back and reflect upon the future of any relationship with him. Your eagerness and enthusiasm must be balanced by the common sense of a businessman.

Will your franchisor provide you with what you need and will you be able to conform to his expectations?

Here, let me give you an example of a relationship which did not work out so well.

Another of my sons, also experienced in the family business, was eager to take up a franchise.

Andy, unlike Tim, did not want a business where he potentially would be employing quite a few people so he opted for a locksmith franchise. After he had an initial meeting with the directors of the company he seemed to think everything was okay, but he was being driven by the wrong motives to buy. He had thought it through and on the face of it he was going in the right direction, choosing a hands-on franchise which suited his needs and strengths but because he wanted to do it far too quickly he did not check out the facts and information he had been given.

One cardinal sin he will never commit again was not contacting existing franchisees other than the ones given by the franchisor. He was given his training, which he felt was satisfactory, his new leased van was fully equipped with stock, tools, and key-cutting equipment and off he went in to the bright blue world of working for himself.

Now don't forget Andy had worked in the business with his older brother Tim, so he knew a bit more than the average about some of the problems that can arise day to day. His expectations of the franchisor were no greater than those that had been set out by them, but there was little or no back-up and they were charging a monthly management fee of £150, so they got that regardless of Andy getting any work.

During the following 12-18 months things did not improve. In fact he had only received three or four referrals from them so the whole of his turnover was down to his own efforts. In marketing and sales, apart from the initial training, you would not have known he had invested in a franchise.

The franchise made no effort whatsoever in arranging sales courses, marketing, IT, advertising, health and safety, or anything to do with the industry in which they were working.

There had been little, virtually nil, contact with him during this period of time, so there was little point in him carrying on paying for something which he was not getting, so Andy dropped their name, which had been of no advantage anyway, and carried on as a sole trader.

Andy made a success of his business, in spite of, not *because* of, the franchisor, so do not let this happen to you. Do your homework and use this book as a check list, making notes as you go along. That's why the notes pages are there!

It is worthwhile bearing this in mind when looking at the different companies you will no doubt come across.

It stands to reason that if a franchisor is only making money when you are turning money over, it is always in their interest to ensure that you are running your business in a proper and professional manner and, very importantly, successfully.

If they are earning money regardless of your success or failure, the less ethical ones will merely sit back and let you suffer.

Another important difference between the two franchises was Driver Hire was and is a member of the British Franchise Association and the one Andy chose was not.

They could make (and break) their own rules with impunity.

So it is vital that you consider not only your qualities but those of your prospective partner before committing yourself.

A good working relationship with your franchisor is the key to success.

The Contract

The franchise agreement or contract sets out the terms and conditions under which you will be allowed to operate and should also include the obligations of the franchisor in respect of your business.

All being well, there will not be any need for either party to bring the document into play providing both are living up to their expectations. Any disputes should be settled informally rather than by wielding the big stick of a contract and only in extremis should it be necessary to take the document out of the file.

Reputable franchisors will have fine-tuned their agreement and there should be few worries on that score. However, it is an important document and if any doubt exists over any of the provisos, recourse should be made to a lawyer familiar with the business. The British Franchise Association has a register of suitably qualified solicitors.

There are three principal functions of an agreement.

- Firstly, to have in writing the generally agreed principles for the relationship to avoid disputes arising at a later date
- Secondly, to preserve the right of the franchisor in respect of his know-how, trademarks and trade secrets etc
- Lastly, to set out the terms of the relationship between the two parties, the rules that both will abide by.

A reputable franchisor will ensure that every one of his franchisees receives an identical agreement. If, for instance, you were to be offered a 'special deal' it would be cause for some concern. Who knows what other 'special deals' might have been negotiated with your fellow franchisees. It would be a highly unethical procedure, indicative of the franchisor trying to make a sale at all costs.

And should news of such an agreement reach the ears of the other franchisees, there would be, to put it mildly, a good deal of dissatisfaction.

Although the agreements differ in detail from trade to trade, there are some common features.

The initial part of the agreement relates to the purchase of the franchise. It is in effect a good faith agreement, allowing both parties to go ahead with the initial preparations for the marriage, allowing both to research their respective areas of interests to establish that it will be, indeed, a successful partnership.

Undoubtedly you will have had to provide a deposit to get this far and it is important to establish under what conditions such a deposit would be returned should either party decide not to go ahead.

About now you would probably need to prepare a business plan, about which essential ingredients there will be more in the next chapter.

Assuming all is well and both parties are agreed, next comes the Franchise Agreement proper.

This is a far more extensive document and requires a great deal more study of the fine print. As I have said, a well-established franchise will have ironed out all the wrinkles in this but this does not mean that you should not go through it with a fine-toothed comb.

Herein you will find the obligations of the franchisor towards you. Perhaps this might be in the finding of premises or of supplying a vehicle, obtaining a lease on your behalf and negotiation with a landlord.

In return, you have come up with the money and comply with the franchisor's requirements in terms of training etc.

Once signed, sealed and delivered, your obligations become rather more irksome, for the franchisor will be looking to you to get the business off to a flying start on his behalf.

The fine details of the contract will cover the details of the franchise and its trademarks and any patented processes or business secrets. The length of the contract will be stipulated and this should be long enough for the franchisee to establish his business satisfactorily. A period of at least five years would be usual with options for renewal. These should be looked at carefully as they may differ slightly from your original terms, perhaps the franchisor having made some revisions to his operations in the meantime.

Territorial rights will be a major feature and there is an obvious advantage here in having an exclusive territory. It does not, of course, shield you from the competition of a rival franchise but does prevent an internecine war between rival franchisees for the same franchise. But not all franchisors feel this way, fearing that exclusive territories may lead to a franchisee being less proactive than otherwise and thereby not exploiting a potential market to the full.

Your agreement should be **absolutely clear** on this point.

Of great interest will be the fees to be incurred by the franchisee, both initial and recurring, and the terms of their payment.

Often this will be by stages and this should be made perfectly clear by listing the amounts and dates. The details of just what you are paying for must be listed here – for training, for stock, etc.

If, at this stage, you belatedly discover that this franchise was not for you, undoubtedly you would have to reimburse the franchisor all or part of his investment.

Management service fees are a substantial factor and it is important to ensure that you will be getting value for money. You will recall that, in the case of my son Andy's franchise, although he was paying a substantial monthly fee, in his case the franchisor failed to deliver.

The franchisor, for his part, will want to ensure that all is well and will do this by way of spot checks of the books and stock etc. Here the franchisee will be responsible for maintaining accounts to an acceptable standard although many franchises will supply the custom-built computer software for the job.

If there is no management fee involved, the franchisor will receive a percentage on sales and the amount of this must be stipulated together with the conditions under which the amount might be varied in the future.

Finally, there should be some mention of promotion and advertising. If the franchisee is expected to contribute towards this, as is likely, the terms and amounts must be stipulated as well as the uses to which the advertising allotment will be put. For example, will there be local advertising to promote the start-up of your franchise?

In summary, the agreement should comprise all the obligations of the franchisor such as training, supply of equipment, assistance with location and, if a retail operation, the shop-fitting. The supply of manuals and ongoing advice and help including assistance in the keeping of adequate records and accounts should also appear.

For the new franchisee, his obligations are to act in a manner that will reflect favourably on the franchisor and his product or service, to endeavour to increase the franchisor's business and to comply with the requirements as laid out in the manuals.

Maintaining the premises in a fit and proper state and supervision of any staff so they uphold the highest standards of the franchisor and thereby protecting the goodwill of the product mark are other features.

The franchisor must have access to records of the franchisee and the conditions for this access should be stated clearly in the agreement.

If there are any points in the agreement which are not clear, ask for an explanation, as there is no excuse for misunderstandings further down the road.

If you are in any doubt, take professional advice. If your own solicitor is not *au fait* with franchises, the British Franchise Association has a list of suitable qualified lawyers to help you.

Finding the money

Perhaps you are in the fortunate position that we were in, having enough capital from previous enterprises that we had no need to go cap in hand to our friendly high street bank for financing. But in all likelihood, most of you will.

Good franchises don't come cheap and if they do, it's well worth asking yourself why.

One of the overwhelming advantages of buying into a long established and successful franchise is that your bank manager will be happy to see you. He's happy because he is in business and with an established operation it is possible for him to see the results and benefits that will accrue. In other words, he reckons there's a good chance of you not defaulting on any advance he makes to you.

Hence the smile.

But for your part, you will also have to convince him that, although you are going to be in partnership with an established and successful business, you are going to manage any money he is prepared to loan you in a businesslike manner.

He will want to see a business plan.

Now the phase 'business plan' strikes fear into the hearts of many an entrepreneur but it shouldn't. It's only an outline of the way in which you intend to carry on the business and the projected results.

In many cases, it can amount to not much more than one sheet of paper but the more elaborate and extensive the business, naturally the more elaborate and extensive the plan. Because of the enormous range of trades, products and services covered by franchises, it would be impossible to give you a template for a suitable plan but I have included an example at the end of this chapter of the sort of financial information that should be included to give you some idea.

If a large sum of money is involved, almost certainly you would be well advised to consult with your accountant who would be able to prepare the type of documents illustrated.

Provided your proposed franchise is well-established and with a good track record of profitability for its existing franchisees, banks will look favourably on your application. Such is the power of the franchise movement today that almost all will have specialised departments dealing with loans to franchises. Therefore you won't have the difficult and embarrassing problem of explaining what it's all about – the banker will know.

There is much valuable material relating to financing from the British Franchise Association. Many franchisors are not, for various reasons, members of this association and it is possible that one that is will be viewed more favourably by your bankers. Also, many franchisors will be eager to help you – it's in their own best interests to find you the finance.

But suppose you want to buy into a new or start-up franchise. These are often attractive because of the low entry level but it is correspondingly harder to obtain finance for them. With no record of success to back them up, you will need considerably greater powers of persuasion to obtain much in the way of finance without perhaps placing some personal collateral with the bank.

And in this case, a very detailed business plan would be a must. The amount that the bank will lend you may depend upon their assessment of the quality of the franchise but will not be more than 70%, dropping to 50% or less in the case of a relatively new and untried operation. Unlike borrowing money for a capital purchase, such as a house, the bank's interest will come from the revenues you generate and to loan a greater percentage would impose an unrealistic burden.

Do not forget your new venture will require two types of financial capital injected into it:

1. **Fixed capital**. This is the money you need to buy the franchise; it also covers the cost of all of the IT and equipment you require to set up, and the legal fees and costs involved with the acquisition of premises
2. **Working capital**. This is the money you will need to pay your daily and weekly bills, such as rent, heat and light, telephones, wages and so on. This is put in place to keep you going until all of that

money comes rolling in.

Usually the fixed capital is converted into a loan for a specific amount over the fixed period.

The working capital will become your overdraft and it may be that in some instances where the franchise you would like to buy is known to the bank, there may already be a package in place for that particular franchise.

The banks' expertise in the area can be invaluable. Their experience in loaning money goes without saying and they have probably had other franchisees from the industry you are looking at or even the same franchisor. One thing for certain is that they will want you to be as successful as you do, so listen to them.

Lloyds Bank, one of the UK banks specialising in the financing of franchisees, has this to say on the subject:

- When selecting a franchise, the decision on which system should be balanced, with unbiased and factual information.

Full research should be undertaken and the best-suited system established by filtering the information you have gained. The suitability of the franchise will be based on your previous skills, preferred industry sector and whether you wish to be on your own or build a business that will employ others.

- The business plan is a vital document for anyone entering into business. The document is important to the bank in assessing your business idea and in understanding your objectives and projected business performance. You may seek professional advice in drafting the plan, as a bank we will give help and guidance as to what should be included. Support can also come from both Business Link advisors and franchisors who may have a draft template which will make completion easier. Additional information needed in the business plan:

1. The CVs of each of the business owners and key employees
2. What the business does and the market in which it operates, including why its products /service is unique, or has a competitive advantage. It should be included the chosen marketplace and competition that exists
3. How you intend to sell your products/ service and who your customers will be. Your marketing and advertising plan to develop the business to meet the growth projections
4. How the business will operate, detailing location, premises, insurance, staffing, supplies, equipment etc
5. Information technology, stock control, health & safety etc
6. Your objectives for the business, both short and longer term, with analysis of its strengths, weaknesses, opportunities and threats (the SWOT analysis).

• In considering the financial elements of the business plan the following points should be noted:

1. The personal assets and liabilities, as well as the income and expenditure of each of the business

owners. The plan should detail your stake in the business and how it was raised. Contribution may come from savings, inheritance, or from a re-mortgage of your residential home. The security you are prepared to offer to the lender to support the finance required

2. Gearing is the ration between funds you borrow and the cash stake in the business. You may need to raise as much as 30-50% of the set-up costs, including the working capital requirement from your own resources. Whilst most banks will lend up to 70% of the total cost of joining a selected well-established franchise system, this is not an option that is automatically available. The bank's decision will depend on the ability of the business to generate sufficient revenue to service your level of borrowing. The more that can be injected into the business, the lower the level of borrowing, which will impact on the financial repayments and interest on the debt

3. Cash flow forecast is the capability of the business to generate cash and it is critical to any business. A well prepared cash flow is vital to any business plan and will tell you when payments have to be made and when income is projected to be received. If the business cannot generate enough cash at the right time to meet its payments there will be a potential problem. Banks can consider cash flow support through overdraft facilities or in certain instances factoring or invoice discounting may be an option to improve cash flow

4. The profit and loss forecast will show the level of profits you expect your business to achieve at the end of a 12-month trading cycle. It will give you details of your sales forecast and set

out all your start-up and operating costs. It is important to stress that the cash flow and profit are not the same thing. It is important that the projections are realistic and it is advisable to speak to other franchisees to establish whether they have found the figures to be achievable. You will need to ascertain whether these franchisees are operating comparable business to that which you are planning in terms of size, premises, territory and staff. You also need to establish whether their level of drawings is similar to our own. They may, for example, be single and living with their parents with a minimal requirement of drawings, while you may have a partner, young family, large mortgage and personal financial commitments. It is also advisable to have some funds to fall back on should the business be unable to reach the forecasted level of sales or, indeed, if costs and overheads exceed their original projections.

In conclusion all too often business plans are given a great deal of attention when people are looking for their initial finance and then not looked at again. The plan should however, always be treated as a working document and not allowed to gather dust. You should make regular comparisons of your business performance against the plan to check your progress. As the business develops the plan should be updated. If at a later date you need additional finance, an updated plan will demonstrate that you have your finger on the financial pulse. The franchisor will often review your business performance on a regular basis, as at the end of the day, their success depends on your own success.

Your bankers or accountants will be more than happy to assist you in the preparation of a suitable business plan.

The Bottom Line-

Keep an eye on it!

What everyone must be very, very aware of, in any business venture not just franchising, is the bottom line – the profit – the percentage.

I have seen many instances of businesses which initially have been successful falling into the trap of being turnover driven. There is nothing wrong in increasing turnover, in fact it is one of the main objectives in growing your enterprise but you must never take your eyes off the bottom line.

Sometimes it is inevitable that you may have to reduce your margins, and there are many reasons for doing so, but let me give you an example of one which we can apply to many different types of business.

Let's say you had a franchise in the recruitment sector for supplying temporary office/IT/cleaning staff and you had a client who was part of a national retail chain who you had been successfully dealing with for two or three years, so they had become an established part of your turnover. Let us, for argument's sale, assume you have been trading with them on a gross profit margin of between 34% and 38%. They, out of the blue, call you to a meeting and inform you that their head office has taken a decision to take control away from their regional stores regarding the outsourcing of the temporary staff.

The plan of head office is a simple one. Rather than having numerous stores dealing with dozens of different suppliers of temporary staff, they will boil the whole thing down to two national companies who will deal directly with the individual stores but for these companies to have this national contract they would obviously have to agree a national rate which would have to reflect he fact that they would be just one of two and not competing with many.

What this *does* mean however is that this contract reflects in the future value in terms of invoicing. In the past when you were dealing directly with the individual stores your gross profit was somewhere between 33% and 38% but now it will be around the 21% to 27% mark. So what do you do?

Well first of all, don't panic. Lay out all of the facts.

1. If you had set up business on your own and not invested in a franchise you would not be part of a national organisation and you would now be doing no business at all with this particular customer.
2. Split the workforce, easing the pain. Leave a few there and try to place the others in more profitable

areas.

3. Accept it but don't forget after you pay your management fee of say 10% your gross profit (GP) becomes 11% to 17%.
4. Pull them out but unless you can place them elsewhere, consider this move very carefully. If it is an ongoing business then you will know roughly how much turnover you will do because of your dealings with them over the last couple of years. It should increase if you are one of only two suppliers.

Weigh up all of your options and discuss it with your regional representative of the franchise. Speak to other franchisees within your organisation; you never know whether they may have different ideas that you have not considered.

While I am sitting her at my computer I absolutely guarantee I could ring my son Tim and he could tell me exactly what gross profit on any business we have done today or yesterday, or any invoices we have sent and, just as importantly, what the gross profit will be on all work that is booked in for the future.

This is what I mean by keeping an eye on the bottom line. There will be times when you think to yourself that the margin has been reduced to a level that you do not want to carry on, but there is a difference between not wanting to and committing commercial suicide. You must weigh everything up, measure what impact it will have overall, right across the business.

Believe you me, I have seen people who run their own business take on work because it has been volume and they have assumed they would be in profit, but because it was high turnover it has taken them longer to recognise the fact that they were actually losing money.

Turnover is obviously of prime importance but turnover alone will eventually run dry if you have not got sufficient margin in place.

An exit strategy

When you set sail on your voyage of many discoveries, the last thing on your mind is EXIT. It means nothing and even as you read this you may be thinking to yourself, he's lost the plot.

Well, read on. It will only take you a few minutes but it may well plant a tiny seed in your memory bank that could be extremely useful to you as you work to make a success of your business. After a few years of enjoying the many varied challenges you will have manoeuvred your way through, by now you will be comfortable with the knowledge that the decisions you made when weighing up all of the pros and cons of buying the franchise were the correct ones.

It may be now you want to take your foot off the pedal a little bit, maybe you even have thoughts about selling your business; some franchisors have departments set up specifically for this reason; because they obviously have a vested interest in whoever is going to become part of their business family. If they do not have a dedicated department they will have a manager or director whose responsibility it is.

Selling your business can be a difficult decision to take because after all it has been a big part of you and no doubt your family life for some time. Let's say you sell, well, there *is* life after; what do you do? A lot depends on how much money you manage to sell your business for and how much is left after our much-loved Inland Revenue has taken its share. On the subject of the Inland Revenue, and completely digressing from the subject that I am addressing, I always stress to people who are asking me for my advice, keep all of your books and records completely up to date, never rely on memory, get the bit of paper, file it and *then* you can forget it. Either you or a member of your family should quickly get up to speed on book-keeping or employ a part-time professional book-keeper and increase their hours as the business grows.

Give all of this information to your accountant, listen to his advice, and ask him what he thinks you should be doing next year that you have not done this year. Then, and this it the tough bit, when the bill arrives from the Inland Revenue – Pay It! Don't listen to those unqualified individuals who give you advice out of their little box of tricks on how to not pay all of that money to the Revenue, pure genius that they are, my advice is... PAY YOUR BILLS AND GET RICH SLOWER.

Anyway back to the plot.

One of the problems in making your decision as to whether to sell the business or carry on is the rather obvious one of how much you will get and when. Before we address those points let us have a think as to WHY we would be contemplating selling.

I could write pages and pages on reasons, but there are only a few that really matter.

I have to assume that the business is making a reasonable profit.

So to the reasons:

You simply have had enough – the buzz has gone, you are not enjoying it in the way you have in the past, it may be that during the years you spent building it up, your eyes have been opened up to other things in life: your family, hobbies and interests you never thought you would become involved in, or you just fancy a complete change or even a new challenge.

Well, unless you intentions are to live on an island, grow your own spuds and catch fish to feed yourselves, you will still be in need of money, so back to the point in question: do you sell?

One of the simplest calculations to do is find out the value of the business (this can be done with the help of your franchisor and your accountant or a business transfer agent). So take the amount your accountant estimates you would be left with after tax and other expenses have been allowed for, and take the simplest of investments, say a bank/building society account.

There are of course other investment vehicles but for our purposes this is a quick and safe route to look at. It may be that you are looking to move to another type of business and the money you would receive from the sale would be sufficient to set you up. If this is the case then you have achieved your goal and you are now ready to set sail to new horizons.

On the other hand it may be you are feeling that you would like to have more time to do all those things you had in mind when the idea of franchising enthused you into being brave enough to pass a cheque over to people who were then complete strangers, and have now become colleagues.

So if you do not sell what are the other options?

KEEP THE BUSINESS and delegate, but with a slight difference. One major problem with delegating is the obvious one, and that is whoever you are asking to do this will at some stage, probably sooner than later, get fed up with 'doing all of the work' and you taking the money, even if you thought about this and paid what you genuinely thought to be fair salary.

The slight difference I mentioned earlier...it's a bit more than slight, but it ticks everyone's boxes. You first of all decide whether you are going to include everyone in this. I should think you will have in mind what I would class as a person you regard as key to your business.

This member, or members, of your team would have attended the training courses set up by your franchisor and they would also have taken on board your personal take on running the business.

Some businessmen, even in the early days, would have an eye to this strategy when employing staff; they would always be considering their options for the future.

Calculate, and be realistic as what you are happy for your basic drawings to be and then quantify that in terms of turnover. So now you know what you have to turn over for you to achieve the income you require to live your life.

Now you are in position to put forward a proposition that will suit everyone. I have seen this work in practice and, if done properly, everyone gains.

Take the monthly turnover that you require and say of that you take a smaller percentage from the profit and the remainder is theirs. You are safe in the knowledge that your income has already been accounted for in the original calculations and as long as the company carries on as it has done historically as far as margins are concerned, things are ok. The win-win situation is there for everyone; you are still involved, albeit in more of a strategic role than you have been before, your chosen team has a golden opportunity to share in the company's financial success, and the franchisor has still got you involved with all of your experience to bring to the table. The team which is now in place has sufficient incentive to put in the effort to grow the company even more than you have done already.

As an added incentive you could also offer to your team that if in the future you were to consider selling the company, they could have first refusal at whatever the market valuation was, less a discount.

It goes without saying that the above manoeuvres must be done with the knowledge and agreement of your partner in the business – your franchisor.

Conclusion

This has been very much a personal story, based upon the experience of myself and my sons in the franchise business.

We have been successful, as you too can be. But if you expect acquiring a franchise is the road to easy riches, don't fool yourself. It requires just as much talent and hard work to be a franchisee as it does to make a success of any other business.

The guidelines I have given you here should enable you to make the right decision both in acquiring your franchise and then running it.

For additional information I cannot do better than to direct you to the British Franchise Association, whether your selected franchisor is a member or not.

Their website contains a wealth of information for both franchisor and franchisee to guide you further.

Bon Voyage!

British Franchise Association

A2 Danebrook Court,
Oxford Office Village,
Langford Lane,
Oxford,
OX5 1LQ
Tel: 01865 379892 Fax: 01865 379 946
www.thebfa.org

Full Members of the bfa.

Accounting and Financial Services

Accountancy & taxation services

Certax Accounting Ltd
47 Clarence Road,
Chesterfield,
Derbyshire, S40 1LQ
www.certaxaccounting.co.uk
Contact:
Mr Keith Bradshaw
Tel: 01246 200255
Fax: 01246 279403
CA@certax.co.uk

DAVIS COLEMAN provides a comprehensive range of services to banks, financial institutions, insurance sector & the legal profession through its network of over 40 offices which cover the whole of England & Wales. Its support services to the banking, insurance and legal professions include: tracing, means/status reports, process serving, commercial debt recovery, repossessions and investigative services.

Davis Coleman Ltd
PO Box 5498,
Ongar,
Essex, CM5 0TJ
Contact:
Mr Harry Varney
Tel: 01277 364333
Fax: 01277 364773
h.varney@daviscoleman.com

Banking, Legal, Insurance Investigators and Consultants

London House (Services) Ltd
London House,
6 The Stocks,
Cosgrove,
Milton Keynes, MK19 7JD England
www.londonhouseservices.co.uk
Contact:
Mr Godfrey Lancashire
Tel: 01908 262 444
Fax: 01908 262 234
info@londonhouseservices.co.uk

Independent Financial Advisers

Money Aspects Ltd
St Andrews House,
385 Hillington Road,
GLASGOW, G52 4BL
Contact:
Mr Andrew Singleton
Tel: 01418 915 999
andrew.singleton@moneyaspects.

co.uk
**Cheque Cashing, Short Term
Loans & Related Financial
Services**

Money Shop
46 Brook Street ,
Chester ,
Cheshire , CH1 3DZ England
Tel: 08453454705
Fax: 08453454715
Contact:
Ms Mary Roberts Tel: 012440565
marie.roberts@dfguk.com

Mortgages

Mortgage Force Ltd
7 Riverside Court,
Pride Park,
DERBY, DE24 8JN
www.mortgageforce.net
Contact:
Mr Nic Lewis
Tel: 0870 8500 780
nicl@mortgageforce.co.uk

TaxAssist Accountants is a white-
collar franchise which spe-
cialises in the supply of accounting,
taxation and associated services to small businesses with a
turnover of under £1million. A
fully-comprehensive training and
support package is provided for
ambitious business builders who
aspire to develop a substantial

accountancy practice. Formal
accountancy qualifications are not
required as full training is provided.
Relevant previous experi-
ence, a good commercial brain and a
desire to succeed are essential.

TaxAssist Accountants
TaxAssist House,
112-114 Thorpe Road,
Norwich, NR1 1RT England
www.taxassist.net
Contact:
The Recruitment Department
Tel: 0800 0188297
Fax: 01603 619992

**Personal searches of residential
properties for the legal sector**

The Property Search Group
Wellington Mills,
70 Plover Road,
Lindley,
Huddersfield, HD3 3HR
Contact:
Ms Geraldine Earnshaw
Tel: 01484 311649
Fax: 01484 311539
geraldineearnshaw@
propertysearchgroup.co.uk

Animal Care

Home from home pet care

Barking Mad Ltd
The Old Stables,
Beckgate Head,
Barbon,
Carnforth, LA6 2LJ
www.barkingmad.uk.com
Contact:
Mrs Lee Southern
Tel: 015242 76476
leesouthern@barkingmad.uk.com

The Complete Pet Care Service -
comprehensive range of
super premium pet food and
accessories with superior service including free home delivery, free
nutritional and behavioural advice from UK experts and free
veterinary support.

Oscar Pet Foods
Bannister Hall Mill,

Higher Walton,
Preston,
Lancashire, PR5 4DB
www.oscars.co.uk
Contact:
Mrs Janet Walmsley
Tel: 01772 647909
discover@oscars.co.uk

Automotive Services

Automotive smart repairs

Advanced Paint Systems T/A
SprayAway
Unit 1, Becklands Park,
York Road,
Market Weighton,
Yorkshire, YO4 3GA England
Tel: 01430 873213
Fax: 01430 871700
www.sprayaway.net
Contact:
Mrs Sharon Louw
Tel: 01430 873213
Fax: 01430 871700
sharonlouw@painta.freeserve.co.uk

Automotive

Autoglym
Works Road,
Letchworth Garden City,
Herts, SG6 1LU

Contact:
Mr Mark Hawthorn
Tel: 01462 677 766
Fax: 01462 686 565
mhaw@autoglym.co.uk

Autosmart International
manufactures and supplies premium quality vehicle cleaning and
maintenance products
direct to the trade via a substantial

network of franchisees from its `one stop shop` mobile showrooms, enabling it to be the `Professionals Choice` for vehicle care products.

Autosmart
Lynn Lane,
Shenstone,
Staffordshire, WS14 0DH
www.autosmart.co.uk
Contact:
Ms Michelle Williams
Tel: 01543 481616
Fax: 01543 481549
franchising@autosmart.co.uk

ChipsAway is the market leader in the SMART (Small to Medium Area Repair Technology) automotive repair sector, providing services to private, corporate and trade clients.

ChipsAway International Ltd
ChipsAway House,
Edwin Avenue,
Hoo Farm Trading Estate,
Kidderminster, Worcestershire,
DY11 7RA
www.chipsaway.co.uk
Contact:
Mr Lloyd Evans
Tel: 01562 825599Fax: 01562 864969
uk@chipsaway.co.uk

etyres is the UK`s leading on-line tyre retailer. With prices 40% lower than leading tyre depots, sales growth is very strong. Can be operated in exclusive territories either as a sole trader or a management franchise.

etyres
Lower Court 3,
Copley Hill Farm Business Park,
Cambridge Road ,
Babraham, CB22 3GN
www.etyres.co.uk
Contact:
Mr Tony Bowman
Tel: 01223 832 444
tbowman@etyres.co.uk

Fast Fit of clutches, gearboxes & brakes

Mr Clutch
2 Priory Road,
Stroud,
Rochester,
Kent, ME2 2EG
Contact:
Stephen Dale
Tel: 01634 717747
Fax: 01634 731115
s.dale@mrclutch.com
Revive! offers a management franchise repairing minor paintwork damage to vehicles (also known as a SMART repair)
Revive! Auto Innovations (UK) Ltd
7 Upton Road,
Rugby,

Warks, CV21 7DL UK
Tel: 01788 569999
Fax: 01788 570080
www.revive-uk.com/franchise
Contact:
Mrs Terry Mullen
Tel: 0800 9174379
Fax: 01788 570080
enquiries@revive-uk.com

Distribution of automotive hand tools

Snap-on Tools
Telford Way,
Kettering,
Northants, NN16 8SN
www.snapon.com/uk
Contact:
Mr. Aldo Rodi
Tel: 01536 413800
Fax: 01536 413900
ukweb@snapon.com

Car & van rental

Thrifty Car Rental
Halifax Road,
Cressex Business Park,
High Wycombe,
Bucks, HP12 3SN
www.thrifty.co.uk
Contact:
Miss Jennifer Singer
Tel: 01494 751500
Fax: 01494 751503
jennifer.singer@thrifty.co.uk

Commercial vehicle power washing

Vendo plc
215 East Lane,
Wembley,
Middlesex , HA0 3NG
Contact:
Mr. I Calhoun
Tel: 0208 908 1234
enquiries@pvcvendo.com

Beauty, Fashion and Health

Hairdressing

Headmasters
145-155 Ewell Road,
Surbiton,
Surrey, KT6 6AW
www.hmhair.co.uk
Contact:
Mr Tim Binnington
Tel: 0208 296 6493
Fax: 0208 241 2198
tim@hmhair.co.uk

Diet & fitness clubs

Rosemary Conley Diet and Fitness
Clubs
Quorn House,
Meeting Street,
Quorn,
Loughborough, Leicestershire,
LE12 8EX
www.rosemary-conley.co.uk
Contact:

Ms Heather Shaw
Tel: 01509 620222
heather.shaw@rosemary-conley.
co.uk

Hair and beauty salons

Saks Hair & Beauty
Saks Franchise Services Ltd,
Saks HQ,
55-59 Duke Street,
Darlington, DL3 7SD
www.saks.co.uk
Contact:
Ms Jennifer Evans
Tel: 01325 380333
Fax: 01325 360228
customerservices@saks.co.uk

Hairdressing

Toni & Guy
Innovia House,
Marish Wharf,
St. Mary`s Road,
Langley, SL3 6DA
Contact:
Ms Gemma Baker
Tel: 01753 612 040
Fax: 01753 612 051
gemma.baker@mascolo.co.uk

Building Maintenance

Portable Appliance Testing and Safety Testing

Calbarrie Ltd
Castle House,
Dawson Road,
Mount Farm,
Bletchley, Milton Keynes, MK1
1QY
Contact:
Mr Spencer Pettit
Tel: 0870 8392806,
Mob: 07771 525414
Fax: 0870 8392802
spencer.pettit@calbarrie.com

Plumbing

Drain Doctor Ltd
Franchise House,
Adam Court,
Newark Road,
Peterborough, Cambridgeshire, PE1
5PP
www.draindoctor.co.uk
Contact:
Mr. F S Mitman
Tel: 01733 753939
jan.mitman@virgin.net

Drain cleaning inspection and repair

Dyno-Rod
Sutherland House,

Maple Road,
Surbiton,
Surrey, KT6 4BJ
www.dyno.com
Contact:
Franchise Recruitment Department
Tel: 0800 316 4604
franchiserecruitment@dyno.com

Lock fitting and security installations

Dyno-Secure
Sutherland House,
Maple Road,
Subriton,
Surrey, KT6 4BJ
www.dyno.com
Contact:
Franchise Recruitment Department
Tel: 0800 316 4604
franchiserecruitment@dyno.com

Commercial Cleaning

Ecocleen Limited
3 Northgate Street,
Bury St Edmunds,
Suffolk, IP33 1HQ
www.ecocleen.com
Contact:
Mr Peter Legge
Tel: 01284 703535
Fax: 01284 700180
atraher@ecocleen.co.uk

Facilities Management

Bricklaying, Joinery, Gardening,
Painting/Decorating, Electrician,
Jointing and Motor Mechanics.
Freedom Group of Companies
Freedom House,
Bradford Road,
Tingley,
Wakefield, WF3 1SD
www.freedom-group.co.uk
Contact:
Ms Michele Glover
Tel: 01924 887785
michele.glover@freedom-group.co.uk
On-site repairs of wood, laminate,
leather upholstery, UPVC,
marble etc for domestic and
commercial customers

Furniture Medic
Tigers Road,
Wigston,
Leicestershire, LE18 4WS
Contact:
Mr Ken Dennis
Tel:0116 2759000
Fax: 0116 2759002
kendennis@servicemaster.co.uk

Safety inspection
gas & electrical equipment &
installations

Gas-Elec Safety Systems Ltd
Brooklyn House,
Money Lane,

The Green,
West Drayton, UB7 7PQ
Contact:
Ms Carol Otway
Tel: 01895 420777
carol.otway@gas-elec.co.uk

Metro Rod offer franchise
opportunities providing drain care
and repair for domestic, commercial
and industrial markets. In
the short-term it is usual that a
franchisee operates as a service
engineer, with the objective of
assuming a management role as
the business develops. Metro Rod
enables each franchisee to
build a profitable business on a
defined territory.
Metro Rod
Metro House,
Churchill Way,
Macclesfield,
Cheshire, SK11 6AY
Tel: 01625 888131
Fax: 01625 616687
www.metrorod.co.uk
Contact:
Mr Alun Mowe
Tel: 0808 2083098
Fax: 01625 616687
franchising@metrorod.co.uk

**Domestic & light commercial
electrical installation & repair**

Mr Electric UK
Five Mile House,
128 Hanbury Road,
Bromsgrove,
Worcestershire, B60 4JZ
Contact:
Mr Clive Houlston
Tel: 01527 574343
Fax: 01527 874031
enquiries@mr-electric.co.uk

**Hydraulic & industrial hoses &
assemblies from depots &
mobiles**

Pirtek Europe plc
35 Acton Park Estate,
The Vale,
Acton,
London, W3 7QE
Contact:
Mr. Alistair Wiggins
Tel: 0208 735 4419
info@pirtek.co.uk

**Refurbishment of flat roofs using
a bonded resin system**

The Flat Roof Company
Unit 7 Guardian Park,
Station Industrial Estate,
Tadcaster,
N Yorks, LS24 9SG
www.flatroof.co.uk
Contact:
Mr. Kevin Moody
Tel: 01937 530788
franchiseinfo@flatroof.co.uk

Renovating and performance upgrading of existing windows using patented system

Ventrolla Ltd
Ventrolla House,
Crimple Court,
Hornbeam Business Park,
Harrogate, HG2 8PB
www.ventrolla.co.uk
Contact:
Mr S C Emmerson
Tel: 01423 859323
Fax: 01423 859321

Business Services

Specialist estate agency board contractors

Agency Express Ltd
The Old Church,
St Matthews Road,
Norwich, NK1 1SP
Contact:
Mr Stephen Watson
Tel: 01603 620044
Fax: 01603 613136
enquiries@agencyexpress.co.uk

Auditel is a leading cost and purchase management franchise.
Working from home, franchisees oversee the acquisition of hundreds of business services. While some have expertise in Auditel's service areas and others have experience at senior management level this is

not essential. A fully comprehensive training and professional development programme is provided to build a substantial practice based on a robust and proven business system.
Auditel
St Pauls Gate,
Cross Street,
Winchester,
Hants, SO23 8SZ
Tel: 01962 863 915
www.auditelfranchise.co.uk
Contact:
Ms Laura Marsh
Tel: 0800 583 3355.
Fax: 01962 854 420
recruitment@auditel.net

Office printer supplies and printer repairs

BIGFISH
Unit A,
Longcamps,
St Sampson,
Guernsey, GY2 4UQ
www.bigfishhooked.com
Contact:
Ms Clare Beer
Tel: 02392 489653
Fax: 02392 472582
clare.beer@bigfishhooked.com

Refill printer cartridges

Cartridge World
Unit A3,
Hornbeam Square West, Hornbeam Park,
Harrogate,
North Yorkshire, HG2 8PA
www.cartridgeworld.co.uk
Contact:
Mr Ben Smith
Tel: 01423 878520
Fax: 01423 878521
ben.smith@cartridgeworld.co.uk

Sell & distribute industrial hygiene, cleaning & maintenance chemicals via mobile showrooms

Chemex International
Hawthorns House,
Halfords Lane,
Smethwick,
West Midlands, B66 1BB
www.chemexfranchises.co.uk
Contact:
Mr Andy Staveley
Tel: 0121 565 6300
Fax: 0121 565 6303
franchiseinfo@chemicalexpress.co.uk

International Franchisees Required

Expense Reduction Analysts, one of the world's largest franchised cost management and value improvement specialists

Expense Reduction Analysts (UK) Ltd.
3 Meridians Cross,
Ocean Way ,
Ocean Village,
Southampton , SO14 3TJ UK
www.erafranchise.net
Contact:
Ms Hayley Lewis
Tel: 0845 0584 771
Fax: 0238 0839 221
h.lewis@erauk.net

Franchise Consultants - International Franchise Consultancy Services

Franchise Development Services - FDS
Franchise House,
56 Surrey Street,
Norwich,
NR1 3FD,
www.fdsfranchise.com
Contact:
Mr Roy Seaman
Tel: 01603 620301
Fax: 01603 630174
roy@fdsltd.com

Short-term rental of personal computers

Hire Intelligence UK
Ilmer Meadows,
Ilmer,
Princes Risborough,

Buckinghamshire, HP27 9RD UK
Tel: 0845 223 9200
Fax: 9845 223 9201
www.hire-intelligence.co.uk
Contact:
Mr Wolf-Rüdiger Feiler
Tel: 0845 223 9200
Fax: 0845 223 9201
wrfeiler@hire-intelligence.co.uk

Personal call answering & messaging service for small business

Kendlebell Ltd
4 Mansfield Business Park,
Lymington Bottom Road,
Medstead,
Hampshire, GU34 5PZ
www.kendlebell.co.uk
Contact:
Mr Simon Carter
Tel: 0844 544 1083
Fax: 0844 544 2447
simon.carter@kendlebell.co.uk

Business, postal & communications services

Mail Boxes Etc
15 Cromwell Park,
Banbury Road,
CHIPPING NORTON, OX7 5SR
www.mbe.co.uk
Contact:
Mr Chris Gillam
Tel: 01608-649230
cgillam@mbe.co.uk

Private investigations bureau

Nationwide Investigations Group
Limited
Clair House,
3-5 Clair Road,
Haywards Heath,
West Sussex, RH16 3DP England
www.investigationfranchise.co.uk
Contact:
Mr. Matthew Thomas
Tel: 0870 417 6667
Fax: 0870 419 9198
contact@investigationfranchise.
co.uk

Management Services

Priority Management
Unit 2, Venture House,
Avro Way,
Bowerhill,
Melksham, SN12 6TD
Contact:
Mr Hugh Dow
Tel: 01225 709533
Fax: 01225 702902

Compact Vending Solutions is designed for businesses with 25-100 employees. SITB, in association with Cadbury, has captured this medium-size market with customers throughout the UK and Ireland who benefit from having snack facilities delivered in a professional reliable and friendly way.

Snack in the Box - Compact
Vending Solutions
Belvedere Point,
Penner Road,
Havant,
Hants, PO9 1QY
www.snackinthebox.co.uk
Contact:
Mr Matthew O`Neil
Tel: 0239 241 5000
Fax: 0239 247 5005
matt@sitb.co.uk

Cleaning of computer equipment

Techclean
Techclean plc,
VDU House,
Old Kiln Lane,
Churt, Farnham, GU10 2JH
Tel: 01428 713713
Fax: 01428 713798
Contact:
Mr. Nick Zarach
Tel: 01428 713 713
Fax: 01428 713798
info@techclean.co.uk

Supply (on sale & rental) of indoor plants, with maintenance service

Urban Planters Franchise Ltd
The Tack Room, The Stables,
Mudgley Road,
Rooks Bridge,
Somerset, BS26 2TH
Tel: 01934 751188

www.urbanplanters.co.uk
Contact:
Mr Nigel Lennard
Tel: 0800 3582245
Fax: 01934 75 11 99
franchise@urbanplanters.co.uk

Cleaning Services

Carpet, upholstery & curtain cleaning service to domestic & commercial customers

Chem-Dry Franchising Ltd
Belprin Road,
Beverley,
East Yorkshire, HU17 0LP
www.chemdry.co.uk
Contact:
Mrs Claire Hostick
Tel: 01482 888195
Fax: 01482 888193
franchise@chemdry.co.uk

Professional domestic oven cleaning service

Cookerburra Oven Cleaning
Services
5/9 Berkeley Avenue,
Reading,
Berkshire, RG1 6EL
www.Cookerburra.co.uk
Contact:
Mr Michael Holloway
Tel: 0118 9599922
Fax: 0118 9595554
Mike@cookerburra.co.uk

Provision of professional domestic cleaning to homes

Merry Maids
Tigers Road,
Wigston,
Leicester, LE18 4WS
Contact:
Mr Ken Dennis
Tel: 0116 2759000
Fax: 0116 2759002
kendennis@servicemaster.co.uk

Management of contract office cleaning services

Minster Services Group UK
Minster House,
948-952 Kingsbury Road,
Erdington,
Birmingham, B24 9PZ
Tel: 0121 3861722
Fax: 0121 3861191
www.minstergroup.co.uk
Contact:
Mr. Mark Huckle
Tel: 0121 386 1722

A management franchise offering a domestic cleaning maid service

Molly Maid UK Limited
Bishop House South,
The Bishop Centre,
Bath Road,
Taplow, Maidenhead, SL6 0NX
http://www.mollymaid.co.uk/
business/index.php
Contact:
Mr Andrew Parsons
Tel: 01628 663500
Fax: 01628 663700
aparsons@mollymaid.co.uk

OVENU, trading throughout the UK and overseas including the USA, offers a van-based and home-managed franchise opportunity offering the highest quality oven cleaning and oven valeting to both the residential cleaning and the semi-commercial sector using caustic-soda free products. Initially dealing directly with clients on a B2C basis but with the opportunity to expand into a true management business franchise over time.
Ovenu
Unit 3,
Station Industrial Estate,
Oxford Road,
Wokingham, RG41 2YQ
www.ovenu.co.uk/oven-cleaning-franchise.cfm
Contact:
Mr Rik Hallewell
Tel: 01189 743911
Fax: 01189 743912
rik.ovenu@ukonline.co.u

The supply of maintenance services for soft furnishings and disaster restoration

Resale opportunities available, please contact Hugh Stoddart Rainbow International Carpet Care and Restoration Specialist
Spectrum House,
Lower Oakham Way,
Oakham Business Park,
Mansfield , NG18 5BY UK
Tel: 01623 675100
Fax: 01623 422466
www.rainbow-int.co.uk
Contact:
Mr. Hugh Stoddart
Tel: 01623 675100
Fax: 01623 422466
h.stoddart@rainbow-int.co.uk

Professional furniture care & expert spot stain removal

Safeclean
152 Milton Park ,
Abingdon ,
Oxon, OX14 4SD
Contact:
Mr. Paul Fennell
Tel: 01235 444757
safeclean@valspar.com

Professional cleaning services for commercial domestic & in-surance customers. Furnishing and carpet repairs & restoration.
ServiceMaster Ltd

ServiceMaster House,
Tigers Road,
Wigston,
Leicestershire, LE18 4WS U.K.
Tel: 0116 275 9000
Fax: 0116 275 9002
Contact:
Mr. Ken Dennis
Tel: 0116 275 9000
Fax: 0116 275 9002
kendennis@servicemaster.co.uk

International Franchisees Required

Hard floor, carpet & upholstery cleaning for national and local commercial and domestic customers.

Stainbusters Ltd
15 Windmill Avenue,
Woolpit Business Park,
Woolpit,
Bury St Edmunds, Suffolk, IP30 9UP
www.stainbusters.co.uk
Contact:
Ms. Christine Gooch
Tel: 0800 137772
franchise@stainbusters.co.uk

Multi-award winning management franchise providing a unique specialist weekly washroom sanitation service and prod-ucts to commercial customers and public sector buildings.

Swisher Hygiene Services UK Ltd
(SHS)
9 Churchill Court,
33 Palmerston Road,
Bournemouth, BH1 4HN UK
Tel: 01202 30 33 33
Fax: 01202 30 32 32
www.swisher.co.uk
Contact:
Ms Donna Hollingworth
Tel: 01202 303333
Fax: 01202 303232
donna@swisher.co.uk

Direct Selling and Distribution

Greeting card publisher distributing through network of franchisees

Card Connection
Park House,
South Street,
Farnham,
Surrey, GU9 7QQ
www.card-connection.co.uk
Contact:
Ms Cynthia Shelton
Tel: 01252 892 391
cynthia-shelton@card-connection.co.uk

Distribution of greetings cards

Card Line Greetings Ltd
Unit 2 Ionic Park,
Birmingham New Road,

Dudley,
West Midlands, DY1 4SJ
www.cardline.co.uk
Contact:
Mr. M Crapper
Tel: 0121 522 4407
Fax: 0121 522 4417
info@cardline.co.uk

Distribution of milk & dairy products & soft drinks

Dairy Crest
14/40 Victoria Road,
Aldershot,
Hampshire, GU1 1TH
www.milkdeliveries.co.uk
Contact:
Mr. Robert Fowler
Tel: 01252 366807
robert.fowler@dairycrest.co.uk

Preservation of wedding bouquets & other floral tributes

Flowers Forever
Sterling House,
10G Buntsford Park Road,
Bromsgrove,
Worcestershire, B60 3DX UK
www.flowersforever.co.uk
Contact:
Ms Hilary Jones
Tel: 01527 880 200
Fax: 01527 880 201
franchising@flowersforever.co.uk

Home delivery of organic vegetable boxes

Riverford Organic Vegetables Ltd
Wash Barn,
Buckfastleigh,
Devon, TQ11 0LD
Tel: 01803 762720
Fax: 01803 762718
www.riverford.co.uk
Mr Ian Bradley
Tel: 01803 762720
Fax: 01803 762718
franchise@riverford.co.uk

SITB has been delivering snacks to the workplace since 1991.
Typically servicing clients with 2-20 staff with a self -service
box. Providing snack facilities in a professional, reliable and
friendly way, along with strong Cadbury marketing support, has
been the key to the SITB success story.
Snack in the Box – Self-Service Box
Belvedere Point,
Penner Road,
Havant,
Hants, PO9 1QY
www.snackinthebox.co.uk
Contact:
Mr Matthew O`Neil
Tel: 0239 241 5000
Fax: 0239 247 5005
matt@sitb.co.uk

Distribution of greeting cards

The Original Poster Company
Elephant House,
28 Lyon Road,
Walton on Thames,
Surrey, KT12 3PU
Tel: 01932 267300
www.originalposter.com
Contact:
Mr Phil Harrison
Tel: 01932 267300
Fax: 01932 267333
mail@originalposter.com

Domestic and Personal Services

Abacus Care
Ormskirk Business Park,
71/73 New Court Way,
Ormskirk, L39 2YT
Tel: 01695 585 400
Fax: 01695 585 401
Contact:
Mr Nigel Fielding
Tel: 01695 585400
Fax: 01695 585401
headoffice@abacuscare.co.uk

Provision of domiciliary care services

Carewatch Care Services Ltd
First Floor,
1 Queen`s Square ,
Brighton, BN1 3FD
Contact:

Mr Michael Miles
Tel: 01273 208111
Fax: 01273 204111
centralsupport@carewatch.co.uk

Domicilary Care Services
Guardian Homecare (UK) Ltd
Unit 7 Coldharbour,
Pinnacles Estate,
Lovet Road,
Harlow, Essex, CM 19 5JL
Contact:
Mr Pat Thompson
Tel: 01992 575666
Fax: 01992 575152
PThompson@clinovia.co.uk

Educational Services

Music Tuition

Clive`s Easylearn Pop Music
Schools
Clive`s Franchise Ltd,
PO Box 305,
Brockenhurst, SO42 7XX UK
Tel: 01590 623162
www.clivesmusic.com
Contact:
Mr Clive Brooks
Tel: 01590 623162
franchise@clivesmusic.com

Music & singing club for pre-school children

Jo Jingles Limited
1 Bois Moor Road,

Chesham,
Buckinghamshire, HP5 1SH
Tel: 01494 778989
Fax: 01494 770729
Contact:
Mrs Gill Thomas
Tel: 01494 778989
Fax: 01494 770729
headoffice@jojingles.co.uk

Education (After-School
Programme Based On Maths And
English)
Kumon Educational UK
5th Floor,
The Grange,
100 High Street,
London, N14 6BN United
Kingdom
Contact:
Mr Dan Alway
Tel: 020 8447 9020
Fax: 0208 8447 9030
instructor@kumon.co.uk

Music and singing classes for pre-school children

Monkey Music
Unit 8,
Thrales End Farm,
Thrales End Lane,
Harpenden, AL5 3NS
www.monkeymusic.co.uk
Contact:
Mrs Carmel Grovestock
Tel: 01582 469242
Fax: 01582 469600

jointheteam@monkeymusic.co.uk

Part-time weekend sports schools for children

SportsCoach
The Courthouse,
Elm Grove,
Walton-On-Thames,
Surrey, KT12 1LZ
www.sportscoach.co.uk
Contact:
Mr Jon Bennetts
Tel: 01932 256262
Fax: 01932 256210
info@sportscoach.co.uk

Part-time theatre schools for children aged 6 - 16

Stagecoach Theatre Arts
The Courthouse,
Elm Grove,
Walton-on-Thames,
Surrey, KT12 1LZ
www.stagecoach.co.uk
Contact:
Mr Manzoor Ishani
Tel: 01932 254333
Fax: 01932 256227
mail@stagecoach.co.uk

Active physical play for pre-school children, in a structured and supervised environment
Tumble Tots (UK) Limited
Bluebird Park,
Bromsgrove Road,

Hunnington,
Halesowen, West Midlands, B62 0TT
www.tumbletots.com
Contact:
Mr David Hunt
Tel: 0121 585 7003
Fax: 0121 585 6891
david.hunt@tumbletots.com

Employment and Training

Nursing and Care Staff Agency

Care@ Bradford Court,
123 - 131 Bradford Street,
Digbeth,
Birmingham, B12 0NS UK
Tel: 0121 693 2470
Fax: 0121 693 2469
www.careat.co.uk/franchising
Contact:
Mr Philip Rainsford
Tel: 0121 693 2470
Fax: 0121 693 2469
admin@careat.co.uk

Executive Recruitment and Management Consultancy

CNA International
4 Boundary Court,
Willow Farm Business Park,
Castle Donington,
Derby, DE74 2UD UK
Tel: 01332 856200
Fax: 01332 856222
www.cnacareers.co.uk

Contact:
Ms Paula Reed
Tel: 01332 856200
Fax: 01332 856222
info@cnainternational.co.uk

International Franchisees Required

Management franchise in the business-to-business arena. Specialise in the recruitment and supply of drivers and logistics staff to the private and public sectors across the UK and Ireland.
Driver Hire
Progress House,
Castlefields Lane,
Bingley ,
West Yorkshire , BD16 2AB
www.driver-hire.co.uk
Contact:
Mr John Warren
Tel: 01274 551166
john.warren@driver-hire.co.uk

Leadership & management training

Leadership Management (UK) Ltd
10 Lake End Court,
Taplow Road,
Near Maidenhead,
Berkshire, SL6 0JQ UK
Contact:
Mr Ray King
Tel: 01628 669888
Fax: 01628 669875

info@lmi-uk.com

IT and Business Skills Training Centres
Pitman Training Group
Sandown House,
Sandbeck Way,
Wetherby,
West Yorkshire, LS22 7DN
www.pitman-training.co.uk
Contact:
Mr. M Cressey
Tel: 01937 548562
franchising-opportunities@pitman-training.com

Recruitment consultancy

Select Appointments plc
Regent Court,
Laporte Way,
Beds, LU4 8SB
www.selectfranchise.co.uk
Contact:
Debbie Smith
Tel: 01582 811600
Fax: 01582 811611
franchise@select.co.uk

Business employment agency

Travail Employment Group Ltd
24 Southgate Street,
Gloucester, GL1 2DP
www.travail.co.uk
Contact:
Mr. Bill Hendrie
Tel: 01452 420700

franchise@travail.co.uk

Estate Agents and Property Management

Bairstow Eves Countrywide

Bairstow Eves Franchising
Century House,
Rosemount Avenue,
West Byfleet,
Surrey, KT14 6LB
Tel: 01932 350314
www.bairstowevesfranchising.co
.uk
Contact:
Network Development Team
Tel: 01932 350314
Fax: 01932 350587
enquiries@bairstowevesfranchising.
co.uk

Property management & residential letting

Belvoir Lettings
The Old Court House,
60a London Road,
Grantham,
Lincoln, NG31 6HR
Tel: 01476 570000
Fax: 01476 584902
www.belvoirfranchise.com
Contact:
Miss Emma Swallow
Tel: 01476 570 000
Fax: 01476 584902
franchising@belvoirlettings.com

Residential property management and lettings agent

Castle Estates
Castle House,
Dawson Road,
Mount Farm,
Bletchley, Milton Keynes, MK1
1QY
www.franchise.castle-estates.co.uk
Contact:
Ms Samantha Knight
Tel: 0870 839 2747
Fax: 0870 839 2728
franchise@castle-estates.co.uk

Country Properties. Established in
1974 and a track record in
estate agency (sales & lettings)
franchising for over 25 years,
its formula and systems have been
tried and tested through
good times and bad. The strength
of brand and its ability to
evoke a positive response amongst
its target audience is an asset
of almost incalculable value.
Country Properties
Head Office,
41 High Street,
Baldock,
Hertfordshire, SG7 6BG
www.country-properties.co.uk
Tel: 01462 896148
Fax: 01462 895123
headoffice@country-properties.
co.uk

Estate agency board suppliers & contractors

Countrywide Signs Limited
PO BOX 163,
Dullingham,
Newmarket, CB8 9UW UK
www.countrywidesigns.com
Contact:
Mr John Ball
Tel: 0870 850 2959
sales@countrywide-signs.com

Property Management & Lettings

Martin & Co.
182 Old Christchurch Road,
Bournemouth, BH1 1NU
www.propertyfranchise.co.uk
Contact:
Franchise enquiries
Tel: 01202 292829
propertyfranchise@martinco.com

Residential lettings

Northwood GB Ltd
1 Bellevue Road,
Southampton, SO15 2AW
Tel: 02380 336677
Fax: 02380 333789
www.northwoodfranchises.co.uk
Contact:
Mr Andrew Goodson
Tel: 02380 336677
Fax: 02380 333789
sales@northwoodfranchises.co.uk

Estate Agency, Lettings, Sales & Management

Xperience - A Network of
Franchised Estate Agents
4 Brewery Court,
43-45 High Street,
Theale,
Reading, RG7 5AJ
www.xperience.co.uk
Contact:
Mr Michael Stoop
Tel: 0845 337 0220
Fax: 0845 337 0221
admin@xperience.co.uk

Fast Food and Catering Services

Specialist coffee, muffins & baguette retail outlet

BB`s Coffee & Muffins Limited
Europa House,
Second Floor,
Church Street,
Middx, TW7 6DA UK
Tel: 020 8758 1234
Fax: 020 8568 6868
Contact:
Mr N Sidhu
Tel: 020 87581234
Fax: 020 8568 6868
franchise@bbscoffeeandmuffins.com

Home delivery and takeaway pizza

Domino`s Pizza
Lasborough Road,
Kingston,
Milton Keynes, MK10 0AB
Contact:
Ms Dawn Power
Tel: 01908 580617
dawn.power@dominos.co.uk

Fast food

Favorite Fried Chicken Limited
7 Davy Road,
Gorse Lane,
Clacton-on-Sea,
Essex, CO15 4XD
Tel: 01255 222568
Fax: 01255 430423
Contact:
Tara Yates
Tel: 01255 222568
Fax: 01255 430423
franchising@favorite.co.uk

Quick service food restaurant

McDonald`s
11-59 High Road,
East Finchley,
London, N2 8AW
Contact:
Franchising Team
Tel: 0208 2714424
Fax: 0208 7007053
franchise@uk.mcd.com

Sandwich Cafe

O`Briens Irish Sandwich Bars
2 Elsinore House,
77 Fulham Palace Road,
London , W6 8JA
www.obriens.ie
Contact:
Mr Paul Stanton
Tel: 0208 741 7777
Fax: 0208 741 7788
info@obriens.ie

A world-class brand, Papa John's
is one of the most exciting,
fastest expanding pizza companies
having opened over 3,000
stores worldwide – with a ground-
breaking new UK store design
that sets it apart from all other pizza
delivery and takeaway operations. Papa John's pledge is "better
ingredients, better pizza"
and it is this motto that sets the
standard for the premium quality
customers have come to expect
from the brand.
Papa John's (GB) Limited
Units 5 & 6 The Forum,
Hanworth Lane,
Chertsey ,
Surrey, KT16 9JX
www.papajohns.co.uk
Contact:
Ms Armanda Jarvis
Tel: 01932 568000
armanda_jarvis@papajohns.co.uk

Fast food restaurants based on baked potatoes with large variety of fillings

Spud U Like Ltd
9 Central Business Centre,
Great Central Way,
London, NW10 0UR
Contact:
Mr. T Schleisinger
Tel: 0208 8302424
headoffice@spudulike.com

Fast food sandwich outlets
Subway
3 Market Place,
Carrickfergus,
County Antrim,
Northern Ireland, BT38 7AW
www.subway.co.uk
Contact:
Mr Paul Heyes
Tel: 0800 0855058 (UK), 0044 2893 359 080 (Eire)
Fax: 02893 359102
sharp.pencil@dnet.co.uk

Private home meals delivery service

Wiltshire Farm Foods
apetito Ltd,
Canal Road,
Trowbridge,
Wiltshire, BA14 8RJ
www.wiltshirefarmfoods.com
Contact:
Mr Ben Haynes

Tel: 01225 756015
Fax: 01225 756069
ben.haynes@apetito.co.uk

Family hamburger restaurant

Wimpy International Ltd
2 The Listons,
Liston Road,
Marlow,
Buckinghamshire, SL7 1FD
www.wimpy.uk.com
Contact:
Mr. Chris Woolfenden
Tel: 01628 891655
info@wimpy.uk.com

Garden and Landscape Services

Amenity & industrial weed control services

Complete Weed Control
Suite 7, Corn Mill Bank Offices,
Hinton-on-the-Green,
Evesham,
Worcester, WR11 2QU UK
Tel: 01386 446856
Fax: 01386 45921
Contact:
Mr Ian Graham
Tel: 01386 446856
Fax: 01386 45921
cwcheadoffice@cwc.uk.com

Grounds maintenance contractors

Countrywide Grounds Maintenance
Countrywide House, Oak Green,
Earl Road,
Cheadle Hulme,
Cheshire, SK8 6QL UK
Tel: 0161 485 6666
Fax: 0161 485 8686
www.countrywidegrounds.com/franchise
Contact:
Mr John Kilbey
Tel: 0161 485 6666
Fax: 0161 485 8686
franchise@countrywidegrounds.co.uk

Specialised Lawn Treatment

Countrywide Lawn Doctor Ltd
Countrywide House, Oak Green,
Earl Road,
Cheadle Hulme,
Cheshire, SK8 6QL
www.countrywidelawndoctor.com/franchise
Contact:
Mr John Kilbey
Tel: 0161 485 6666
Fax: 0161 485 8686
franchise@countrywidelawndoctor.com

Domestic lawn treatment service

Greenthumb Lawn Treatment
Service
Integra,
St Asaph Business Park,
St Asaph,
Denbighshire, LL17 OJD
Tel: 01745 586062
Fax: 01745 586063
greenthumb.co.uk/the franchise
Contact:
Mr Mark Hallam
Tel: 01745 586062
Fax: 01745 586063
markh@greenthumb.co.uk

Landscape gardening

Scenic Blue
The Plant Centre,
Brogdale,
Brogdale Road,
Faversham, Kent, ME13 8XZ
www.scenicblue.co.uk
Contact:
Mr Phil Gaffer
Tel: 0800 783 3428
Fax: 01795 591059
franchise@scenicblue.co.uk

Tree stump grinding specialists

Stumpbusters UK Ltd
Hill House,
Brimmers Road,
Princes Risborough,
Bucks, HP27 0LE

Contact:
Mr Martin Chignall
Tel: 01844 342851
stump@globalnet.co.uk

Graphic Design and Print

Rapid response print, copy and publishing stores

AlphaGraphics
Providence House,
2 Innovation Close,
York Science Park,
Heslington, York, YO10 5ZF
United Kingdom
Tel: 01904 751080
www.alphagraphics.co.uk
Contact:
Ms Tammy Mitchell
Tel: 01904 751080
info@alphagraphics.co.uk

Business to Business Management Franchise supplying signs and digital print solutions.

Fastsigns
Dunston Innovation Centre,
Dunston Road,
Chesterfield, S41 8NG
franchise.fastsigns.co.uk
Contact:
Mr Garth Allison
Tel: 0800 093 4977
Fax: 01246 261604
sales.uk@fastsigns.co.uk
kristy.millward@fastsigns.com

Quick printing centre offering comprehensive design printing finishing photocopying service
Kall-Kwik UK Ltd
Artemis,
Odyssey Business Park,
West End Road, South Ruislip,
Middlesex, HA4 6QF
www.kallkwik.co.uk
Contact:
Nicky Newman
Tel: 01895 872067
Fax: 01895 872110
franchise.sales@kallkwik.co.uk

Print Design and supply for SMEs

Printing.com
Focal Point,
3rd Avenue, The Village,
Trafford Park,
Manchester, M17 1FG
Contact:
Mr Simon Davies
Tel: 0161 848 5713
simon.davies@printing.com

Fast print centres incorporating artwork & design commercial copying & business communications services
Prontaprint Ltd
Artemis,
Odyssey Business Park,
West End Road, South Ruislip,
Middlesex, HA4 6QF

www.prontaprint.com
Contact:
Mr Craig Johnston
Tel: 08457 626 748
franchisesales@prontaprint.com
Ms Sheri White
Tel: 08457 626 748
franchisesales@prontaprint.com

Sign makers

Signs Express
Franchise Head Office, The Old Church,
St Matthews Road,
Norwich,
Norfolk, NR1 1SP UK
Tel: 0800 7312255
Fax: 01603 613136
www.signsexpress.co.uk
Contact:
Mr. Tony Marsh
Tel: 0800 7312255
Fax: 01603 613136
tony.marsh@signsexpress.co.uk

Hotel, Leisure Industry and Pubs

Public House Retailing

Scottish & Newcastle Pub
Enterprises
2-4 Broadway Place,
South Gyle Broadway,
Edinburgh, EH12 9JZ Scotland,
United Kingdom.

Tel: 07803 798 322
Fax: 0131 528 2889
www.pub-enterprises.co.uk
Contact:
Mr Paul Green
Tel: Freephone 0500 94 95 96
Fax: 0191 224 6357
sophie.baker@pub-enterprises.co.uk

Parcel and Courier Service

Express parcel delivery

ANC
Parkhouse East Industrial Estate,
Chesterton,
Newcastle-under-Lyme,
Staffordshire, ST5 7RB
Tel: 380
www.anc.co.uk
Contact:
Mr John Hamill
Tel: 01782 563322
Fax: 01782 563633
Parcel distribution
Express Despatch
Fairview Industrial Estate,
Kingsbury Road,
Curdworth,
Sutton coldfield, B76 9EE UK
Tel: 01675 475754
www.xdp.co.uk
Contact:
Mr. Louis John
Tel: 01675 475757
admin@xdp.co.uk

Overnight parcels collection & delivery

Interlink Express Parcels Ltd
P.O. Box 6979,
Roebuck Lane,
Smethwick, Warley,
West Midlands, B66 1BY
Contact:
Mr. Mike Noad
Tel: 01562 881002
Fax: 01562 881001
jane.hodgkinson@geopostuk.com

Promotional Products

27 years market leaders in the manufacture, supply and sourcing of personalised name badges, interior and exterior signage, corporate merchandise, business gifts, staff awards and promotional products.
Recognition Express Ltd
Unit 2, Cartwright Way,
Forest Business Park,
Bardon, Coalville ,
Leicestershire, LE67 1UB
www.recognition-express.com
Contact:
Mr. Nigel Toplis
Tel: 01530 513300
Fax: 01530 513309
ntoplis@recognition-express.com

Retail Sales and Shops

Retail opticians
Abbeyfield V.E. Ltd
Abbeyfield Road,
Lenton,
Nottingham, NG7 2SP
Contact:
Mrs Rosaleen Reed
Tel: 0115 988 2109
Fax: 0115 988 2175

Manufacturers & retailers of window blinds to the domestic & commercial markets

Apollo Window Blinds Ltd
unit 102, BMK Industrial Estate,
Wakefield Road,
Liversedge,
West Yorkshire, WF15 6BS
www.apollo-blinds.co.uk
Contact:
Ms Karen Musson
Tel: 01924 413010
Fax: 0871 9892981
karen.apollo1@amoblinds.co.uk
Retail television & hi-fi
Bang & Olufsen
630 Wharfedale Road,
Winnersh Triangle,
Wokingham,

Berks, RG41 5TP
Contact:
Mr D Mottershead
Tel: 0118 969 2288
UKfranchise@bang-olufsen.dk

Retail sale and installation of fires, fireplaces and central heating from high-street showrooms.

Blazes Fireplace and Heating
Centres Limited
23 Standish Street,
Burnley,
Lancs, BB11 1AP
www.blazes.co.uk
Contact:
Mr. M Eyre
Tel: 07000 252 937
enquiries @blazes.co.uk

Food Retail - Convenience Store

Budgens Stores Ltd
Musgrave House, Widewater Place,
Moorhall Road, Harefield,
Uxbridge, Middlesex, UB9 6PE
Contact:
Mr Charles Mills
Tel: 0870 0500158
charles.mills@musgrave.co.uk

Buying & selling high quality second-hand goods
Cash Converters
Cash Converters House,
Westmill Road,

Ware,
Hertfordshire, SG12 0EF
Contact:
Mr Mark Lemmon
Tel: 01920 485696
Fax: 01920 485695
carly.mathura@cashconverters.net

High-street second-hand and new goods retailer. Financial services provided.

Cash Generator
63/64 Oakhill Trading Estate,
Worsley Road North,
Walkden, M28 3PT
www.cashgenerator.co.uk
Contact:
Mr. Robin Page
Tel: 01204 574444
Fax: 01204 577711
info@cashgenerator.co.uk

Retail shoe shops

Clarks Shoes
40 High Street,
Street,
Somerset, BA16 OYA
Contact:
Mr. David Crudge
Tel: 01458 443131
david.crudge@clarks.com

Ladies & gentlemen's hairdressing

Francesco Group
1 The Green,
Stafford, ST17 4BH
Contact:
Mr. Ben Dellicompagni
Tel: 01785 247175
Fax: 01785 216185
emmajohnson@francescogroup.co.uk

Retailers of kitchens and appliances

In-Toto Ltd
Shaw Cross Court,
Shaw Cross Business Park,
Dewsbury,
West Yorkshire, WF12 7RF
www.intotofranchise.co.uk
Contact:
Ms. E Wilson
Tel: 01924 487 900
evelyn.wilson@intoto.co.uk

National school-wear centres, retail, business opportunity.
National Schoolwear Centres plc
Ketteringham Hall,
Church Road,
Wymondham,
Norfolk, NR18 9RS UK
Tel: 01603 819966
Fax: 01603 819977
Contact:
Mr Ian Masson

Tel: 01603 819966
Fax: 01603 819977
ianm@n-sc.co.uk

Golf Retail

Nevada Bob UK Ltd
54 Clarendon Road,
WATFORD, WD17 1DU
Contact:
Mrs Helen Barnish
Tel: 01923 431 624
Fax: 01923 438 063
info@nevadabobs.co.uk

News Agency

Northcliffe Retail Ltd
St George Street,
Leicester, LE1 9FQ
Contact:
Mr Vance Potter
Tel: 01162 224801
Fax: 01162 516802
taramistry@northclifferetail.co.uk

Sale & hire of wedding & bridesmaid dresses & men's formal wear

Pronuptia Bridal & Mens Formal
Wear
PO Box 2478,
Hove, BN3 6AG United Kingdom
Tel: 01273 563006
Fax: 01273 563006
Contact:
Mr Robert Devlin

Tel: 01273 563006
Fax: 01273 563006
pronuptia@btopenworld.com

Television & HiFi

Sevenoaks Sound & Vision
Coleridge House ,
27 New Street,
HENLEY on THAMES,
Oxfordshire , RG9 2BP UK
www.sevenoaksfranchising.co.uk
Contact:
Mr. Malcolm Blockley
Tel: (01491) 636 328
Fax: (01491) 636 328
m.blockley@btconnect.com

Sale & manufacture of fitted bedroom furniture with sliding doors

Sliderobes
Sliderobes House,
61 Boucher Crescent,
Belfast, BT12 6HU Northern
Ireland
Tel: 028 9068 1034
Fax: 028 9066 1032
www.sliderobes.com
Contact:
Mr Rodney Jess
Tel: 028 90 681034
Fax: 028 90 661032
franchise.enquiries@sliderobes.com

The Photo & Digital Specialists on the High Street

Snappy Snaps Franchises Ltd
Glenthorne Mews,
Glenthorne Road,
Hammersmith,
London, W6 OLJ
www.snappysnaps.com
Contact:
Mr. T MacAndrews
Tel: 0208 741 7474
info@snappysnaps.co.uk

Specialist chocolate & sugar confectionery

Thorntons
Franchise / JV Co-ordinator,
Thornton Park,
Somercotes,
Derby, DE55 4XJ
Contact:
Ms Ruth Brown
ruth.brown@thorntons.co.uk
Ms Naomi Bullivant
naomi.bullivant@thorntons.co.uk
Miss Fiona Radford
Tel: 01773 540757
Fax: 01773 540757
fiona.radford@thorntons.co.uk
Mr Han Van Reen
Tel: 01773 542086
Fax: 01773 540757
han.vanreen@thorntons.co.uk

Threshers, Thresher Wine Shop + The Local

Thresher Group
Enjoyment Hall,
Welwyn Garden City,
Hertfordshire, AL7 1BL
www.threshergroupfranchise.com
Contact:
Caroline Gadsby
Tel: 01707 387 428
Fax: 08707 560 639
franchiseregistration@
threshergroup.com

Carpet Retailers

United Carpets Woodfloor & Beds
Waterside House,
Station Road,
Mexborough,
Yorkshire, S64 9AQ
Contact:
Mr David Norman
Tel: 01709 579 450
Fax: 01709 579 448
davidnorman@unitedcarpets.net

Portrait photographers

Venture Portraits
Premier Park,
Road One,
Winsford,
Cheshire, CW7 3PT
www.thisisventure.co.uk
Contact:
Mr Mark Witter

Tel: 01606 558 854
Fax: 01606 559 203
markwitter@thisisventure.co.uk

Banks with Franchise Departments

HSBC
Franchise Unit,
12 Calthorpe Road,
Birmingham, B15 1QZ
www.hsbc.co.uk
Contact:
Cathryn Hayes
Tel: 0121 455 3438
franchiseunit@hsbc.com

Lloyds TSB plc
Business Banking ,
Canon`s House PO Box 112,
Canon`s way,
Bristol, BS99 7LB
http://www.lloydstsbbusiness.com
Contact:
Mr. Richard Holden
Tel: 0117 943 3089
franchising@lloydstsb.co.uk

NatWest
Natwest Franchise Section,
Level 2, 2 Waterhouse Square,
138-142 Holborn,
London, EC1N 2TH
www.natwest.com/franchise
Contact:
Mr Mark Scott
Tel: 0800 092 9117
franchise.retailbanking@natwest.com

The Royal Bank of Scotland plc
RBS Franchise Section,
Level 2, 2 Waterhouse Square,
138-142 Holborn,
London, EC1N 2TH
www.rbs.co.uk
Contact:
Denise Aitchison
Tel: 0800 092 9117
FranchiseRBS.RetailBanking@rbs.co.uk

Franchise Meeting Questionnaire

Franchisor:

Held at:

Date and time:

Present:

1 Are you members of the BFA and if so what type of membership?

If you are not a member, why not? (remember the greatest percentage of franchisors are not members of the BFA.)

2 How long has your company been trading and how long have you been franchising?

3 What is the number of existing franchisees and how do you split areas? By postcode, per head of population, households?

(In some instances it can be beneficial to get involved witha franchise just starting out, because you have the pick ofthe areas available. The franchise purchase fee may befairly low at this stage as well but because it is new it is un-proven as far as franchising is concerned, therefore at maybe a higher risk than an established franchisor. Also, if youneed to borrow from a bank, they will be less favourably in-clined towards a franchisor who has no established recordof success.

4 The training. Where will it take place, in the classroomor in the field? Is it ongoing? Apart from the obvioustraining regarding the product or service, does it cover admininstration, financial management, marketing, ITetc?

5 Do you have a national sales force and what sort ofhelp do I get in my area? Do you open doors on a national head office basis? And then would I be expected

to approach individual regional offices within my area? Apart from your national advertising and literature, am I helped in any other way?

6 Point out a number of areas of the country and ask howlong the franchisees have been with them. Do they turndown many potential new franchisees and if so why?What are they looking for in a new franchisee?

7 Is the area exclusive to me? How long will the franchise agreement run for and how is it renewed? Give me a couple of actual examples. Have you ever refused to renew and why?

8 How much is the initial franchise fee?What is the ongoing management fee?Are there any other fees?

9 Do you have a sample copy of the franchise agree-ment for me to take away and study. (It would be usual atthis stage for you to sign a confidentiality agreement).

10 Do you have a sample forecast of projected turnoverfor the first five years?How about the projected profit for the same period?

11 Can I sell my franchise on the open market and, ifso, can you help? (Remember a successful franchisor will probably have a strong brand, therefore putting you in a good position in the marketplace if you decide to move on). Antother question worth asking is: can you move it on to a close family member?